Portrait of a Survivor

Florence M. Soghoian

*Remembering the past
with hope for the future.
Florence M. Soghoian*

Founded 1910
THE CHRISTOPHER PUBLISHING HOUSE
HANOVER, MASSACHUSETTS 02339

PRINTED IN THE UNITED STATES OF AMERICA

Dedication

For Shnorhig and Vartouhi and all of the other survivors of the Armenian Genocide. And for all of those who died, yet live on forever.

Table of Contents

Prologue

Chapter 1

*The Historical Context of
the Armenian Genocide* 1

Chapter 2

Life Before the Genocide 9

Chapter 3

The Genocide and Death March 19

Chapter 4

Orphanage Life 35

Chapter 5

The Journey to a New World 57

Chapter 6

Early Life in America...................................... 65

Chapter 7

Circles of Love.. 79

Chapter 8

Giving Back in the New World................................. 97

Chapter 9

Family Heirlooms and Other Treasures...................... 107

Chapter 10

The Strength to Survive.. 125

Chapter 11

Living One's Faith....................................... 133

Epilogue.. 145

Bibliography 147

Acknowledgments

I wish to thank all of my family and many of my friends for their help and encouragement in the writing of this book. Particularly, I want to thank my brother Yervant, my sister Rose, and my cousin Steve for their efforts in making this work a reality. I am indebted to each one of them for their caring.

I believe that I began the writing of this work when I wrote my first "book" as a preschooler for my father and mother. Their praises and encouragement were the genesis of all of my creativity that followed.

My deepest appreciation is for Shnorhig and Vartouhi. Had they not been willing to tell their story as eloquently as they did, I would not have been able to transcribe it for them. I am truly honored to have had that privilege.

Florence M. Soghoian

Prologue

My mother's story begins in Zeitoun, a small town in eastern Turkey, once a part of Ancient Armenia. Zeitoun means olive, and so it was in the region of many olive trees that she was born, like her mother before her.

From very ancient times, significant historical events have occurred around the olive tree, from Noah's cautious departure from the Ark, to the classes of Socrates and Plato, and later the betrayal of Christ on Mount Olive. A tenacious tree, it is difficult to destroy. Even the fire and axe of the ancient warrior could not destroy this resilient tree because its strong and pliable wood would not burn easily and it revived itself even after the most violent blows of the warrior's axe. Its heartiness has also enabled the olive tree to survive in drought areas as well.

Always, the olive tree has been able not only to survive extreme adversity, but also in time to flourish once again, bearing fruit for countless generations, its lifespan seemingly having no limits. Many have said of the olive tree that it may suffer, but it will never die.

My mother's story follows.

1

The Historical Context of the Armenian Genocide

My mother's story is one that most people in our society do not know about. It is not taught in history classes in our schools, though perhaps had it been addressed sufficiently, Hitler would not have felt confident enough to say in August of 1939: "Who after all speaks today of the annihilation of the Armenians?" and then proceeded with the holocaust of the Jews. It is a story of the Armenian Genocide, the first genocide in modern times.

Perhaps many of you who are unfamiliar with this part of history are rightfully wondering: Where is Armenia? Who are the Armenians? What is the Armenian Genocide? Why did this horrible genocide happen?

Armenia is perceived by Biblical scholars as being the site of the start of civilization, placing the Garden of Eden there, as well as Noah's Ark landing on Mount Ararat in Armenia. Although this ancient country is presently only about the size of Rhode Island, it was once most of that which is now known as Turkey.

Armenia is the first nation in the world to have accepted Christianity as its national religion, doing so in A.D. 290, 40 years before Emperor Constantine acknowledged Christianity for the Roman Empire. The people in this small, mountainous country refused to give up their Christianity despite centuries of persecution by the Turks, who tried unsuccessfully to convert them to the Islamic faith. During a three decade period, 1894 to 1924, Armenians were systematically uprooted from their homeland of 3,000 years and eliminated through massacres or exile. The years of 1915 through 1924 are known as the Armenian Genocide, when one and a half million Armenians were brutally murdered and more than a half million were exiled from their homes. The Turks believed that they would all eventually perish from torture by the Turkish soldiers, starvation, disease, or exposure.

In the United States Archives, there is an abundance of documentation of the Armenian Genocide, including Senate Resolution 359 on May 13, 1920: "...the testimony adduced at the hearings conducted by the subcommittee of the Senate Committee on Foreign Relations have clearly established the truth of the reported massacres and other atrocities from which the Armenian people have suffered."

Henry Morgenthau, who was then the United States Ambassador to the Ottoman Empire, wrote in his book, *Ambassador Morgenthau's Story*, published in New York in 1918, about the horror of the Armenian Genocide, explicitly describing some of the fiendish techniques of torture of the Armenians by Turkish gendarmes: "...A common practice was to place the prisoner in a room, with two Turks stationed at each end and each side. The examination would then begin with the bastinado. This is a form of torture not uncommon in the Orient; it consists of beating the soles of the feet with a thin rod. At first the pain is not marked; but as the process goes slowly on, it develops into the most terrible agony, the feet swell and burst, and not infrequently, after being submitted to this treatment, they have to be amputated. The gendarmes would bastinado their Armenian victim until he fainted; they would then revive him by sprinkling water on his face and begin again. If this did not succeed in bringing their victim to terms, they had numerous other methods of persuasion. They would pull out his eyebrows and beard almost hair by hair; they would extract his fingernails and toenails; they would apply red-hot irons to his breast, tear off his flesh with red-hot pincers, and then pour boiled butter into the wounds. In some cases the gendarmes would nail hands and feet to pieces of wood — evidently in imitation of the Crucifixion, and then, while the sufferer writhed in his agony, they would cry: 'Now let your Christ come and help you!' "[1]

In his book, Morgenthau discussed his many and varied attempts to convince Turkish officials to put a stop to the horrendous torture and massacre of the Armenian people, documenting further the unspeakable methods of grotesque torture and killing that the Turks were using in their attempt to extinguish the Armenian race: "One day I was discussing these proceedings with a responsible Turkish official, who was describing the tortures inflicted. He made no secret of the fact that the

---

[1]Henry Morgenthau, *Ambassador Morgenthau's Story* (New York: New Age Publishers, 1918), p. 306.

Government had instigated them, and, like all Turks of the official classes, he enthusiastically approved this treatment of the detested race. This official told me that all these details were matters of nightly discussion at the headquarters of the Union and Progress Committee. Each new method of inflicting pain was hailed as a splendid discovery, and the regular attendants were constantly ransacking their brains in the effort to devise some new torment. He told me that they even delved into the records of the Spanish Inquisition and other historic institutions of torture and adopted all the suggestions found there. He did not tell me who carried off the prize in this gruesome competition, but common reputation throughout Armenia gave a pre-eminent infamy to Djevdet Bey, the Vali of Van, whose activities in that section I have already described. All through this country Djevdet was generally known as the 'horsehoer of Bashkale' for this connoisseur in torture had invented what was perhaps the masterpiece of all — that of nailing horseshoes to the feet of his Armenian victims."[2]

Morgenthau continued his discussion of the Turks' plan for the total annihilation of the

---

[2]*Ibid.*, p. 307.

Armenian race as not only violent massacre as its method, but also deportation to the desolate wasteland of the Syrian desert: "...When the Turkish authorities gave the orders for these deportations, they were merely giving the death warrant to a whole race; they understood this well, and, in their conversations with me, they made no particular attempt to conceal the fact."[3]

After pages of graphic descriptions of the grotesque horror of the death march of those Armenians forced to deport from Turkey, Ambassador Morgenthau wrote: "My only reason for relating such dreadful things as this is that, without the details, the English-speaking public cannot understand precisely what this nation is which we call Turkey. I have by no means told the most terrible details, for a complete narration of the sadistic orgies of which these Armenian men and women were the victims can never be printed in an American publication. Whatever crimes the most perverted instincts of the human mind can devise, and whatever refinements of persecution and injustice the most debased imagination can conceive, became the daily misfortunes of this devoted

_____

[3]*Ibid.*, p. 309.

people. I am confident that the whole history of the human race contains no such horrible episode as this. The great massacres and persecutions of the past seem almost insignificant when compared with the sufferings of the Armenian race in 1915."[4]

From Ambassador Morgenthau in 1915 to our leaders in the present time, American Presidents, including Jimmy Carter and Ronald Reagan, U.S. Senators, and other dignitaries have eloquently recognized the shocking truths of the Armenian Genocide. But it is my mother and my grandmother who courageously lived through the horror of it with their spirits intact. The inability of the Turks to defeat their spirit or to destroy their religious and ethical convictions is their eloquence. They are the survivors, and this is their story.

[4]*Ibid.*, p. 321-322.

2

Life Before the Genocide

My mother's story begins on March 14, 1908, when Shnorhig (Armenian for Grace) Keshishian was born in Zeitoun, a town in eastern Turkey, originally a central part of Ancient Armenia. Built on rocky hills and very scenic, this mountainous region was in the province of Aleppo and had a population of less than 25,000 Armenians.

At the age of two her family moved to Marash, a city with a population of about 65,000 residents. It was a thriving city with an American University and a seminary there, as well as many shops, all specialized. For example, there were shops where only meat was sold; others for vegetables or fruits only; sugar, coffee, and candy were found in a speciality shop for imported goods. There one could buy pulverized coffee for Armenian demitasse as well as small sugar cubes; Shnorhig does not remember spoon sugar in her childhood. There were also bakeries and gift shops in this bustling city.

Shnorhig remembers having a very comfortable and happy life in Marash. She lived with her mother, her little sister Rosalia and baby brother Barkev, and her grandparents in a two-story, white stucco house. Her mother, Vartouhi (Kerigian) Keshishian, was well-educated and a nurse. Shnorhig's father, Hovannes Keshishian, did not live with them because he had been conscripted into the Turkish army when she was three years old and was stationed near Constantinople.

Their stucco house was always very white as were the plaster walls within, as they were whitewashed whenever needed. She vividly remembers the Oriental rugs that covered the wooden floors; there were some rugs on the walls too, along with other handmade items. They slept on mattresses upstairs, but she remembers on warm nights they took their mattresses to the roof to sleep; she loved that very much.

Downstairs in their home they had cold running water which ran all of the time as there was no faucet. It came from a stone, tub-like area, though not as large as a tub, but in that shape. As well as being their source of water, it also allowed them a way to preserve meat for a day or so, as the meat could be left in a covered pan, the cold water running over the covered pan, thereby keeping the meat refrigerated.

There was a fireplace in their home where some of the cooking was done on open fire. Sheet bread was made on a big tin that was placed over the fire. They also had a hibachi, where certain dishes were prepared, such as dolma (various vegetables with a filling of either bulghour or meat and rice).

Marash had four seasons, so in the winter it could be very cold, and sometimes there was snow. Though they could get warmth from the fireplace and even the hibachi, they had still another means for warmth when it became very cold. In their home was a frame in the shape of a table with no top; on the coldest of nights a large blanket was thrown on top of the frame, after which the hibachi was centered under the blanket. Everyone would then cluster under the blanket and get warm before going to bed.

Being the first grandchild, Shnorhig was spoiled in wonderful ways by her doting grandparents. She remembers her grandmother, a blond, blue-eyed woman, always treating her in a very special loving way. For example, she often took Shnorhig visiting with her. It was not unusual for her granddaughter to get restless during these visits and tell her that she wanted to go home. With a smile, Shnorhig remembers how her grandmother would then take out the raisins and nuts that she had lovingly stored, for just such an occasion, in the wide belt that she wore and give them to her granddaughter to eat, thus satisfying her for the moment.

Her memories of her grandfather, Mgerdich Keshishian, are even more vivid, as he was a very warm and loving man who treated her as though she were the most precious person in the world. No doubt he was also trying to compensate for the absence of her own father — his son — because he has been forced into the Turkish army before his baby daughter had had a chance to really know her own father. Her grandfather, a shoemaker by trade, had his own shop where Shnorhig remembers his making her very special shoes, which were always the fanciest and prettiest shoes that he made. He also used to carve her flutes, using the hard wood of the mulberry tree. This she loved so very much, perhaps because her grandfather was an expert fiddler and she felt that she could create music with him. It is understandable why Shnorhig didn't feel her father's absence so much, because she was so pampered and loved by her grandparents.

Among Shnorhig's happiest memories are how they spent Saturdays. Every week she went to the bathhouses with her family. Each family had its own day for the baths, and her family's day was Saturday. If you wanted to bathe your children during a day not designated as your family's day at the baths, you would heat water that came from the running water in your home and bathe your children there.

From the time that they left for the bathhouse in the morning until they went to bed that night, it was a truly wonderful day. Shnorhig's eyes even light up now as she remembers and talks about it. Her grandfather would take them there and leave them, as the family day at the baths was for the women and children only. There was some soap for bathing, but it was scarce; their hair was washed with clay. It was an extraordinary experience to be in the hot tubs for hours, as the hot, running water was continuous. Not only did it feel so wonderful and relaxing, but it was also fun for the children, as they would run and play in the tubs with other children from time to time. By late afternoon when it was time to leave, they were very tired and relaxed and ready to go home. Also, they were very hungry and excited, anticipating the delicious meal that awaited them!

Grandfather, who had brought them to the baths in the morning, had done the shopping for the day, as was his practice, and then he had gone back to his shop to work. Before going there, however, he had gone to the butcher to pick up the meat for their shish kabob meal for that evening. That meat he had taken to the baker to have him cook it and then put it into the freshly-baked bread that he had ordered for shish kabob sandwiches. The bakery bread that he ordered each Saturday for the sandwiches was soft and thick, not like the thin bread that they prepared at home each day. He would pick up the women and children in the late afternoon, and then they would go to the baker to pick up the shish kabob sandwiches. The next destination was to go home and feast!

The beverages that they could select from as part of their Saturday feast were varied. Quite often they drank tine, which is madzoon (yogurt) mixed with water. Most often it was drunk cold, though in cold weather it was not unusual to drink it hot. Two other beverages that were enjoyed were a licorice drink or one made of molasses. In the morning you would soak the licorice that you kept at home in water or cook it for awhile. When you returned home from the baths, it was ready to drink. If you wished, you could heat it for a hot drink. Also, a drink made of molasses, heated in the winter, was delicious, too. Finally, a favorite drink in cold weather was hot broth, made from the bones that you got from the butcher when you ordered the meat. The bones were always used to make either stew or meat broth. Sometimes, in fact, they ate their shish kabob sandwiches with a delicious soup of some kind instead of having a beverage. She remembers delicious desserts as well, especially paklava, though honey and molasses were used in making it, not sugar.

As wonderful and happy as life was for Shnor-hig and her family in Marash, she loved just as much the time that they spent at their small country place at their vineyards in Alabash. Each summer was spent there preparing food for the winter months. Not only was there the drying of grapes for raisins, but many other candies were made from dried fruits and fruit juices combined with walnuts. One family favorite was roejig, which is a grape juice and nut roll. The process was to string walnut halves, which was then dipped into grape juice and hung to dry. Roejig was also made with the juice of apricots or pears or other fruits that were available. Another favorite candy that they made was pastegh, which is the drying of the thickened juice of grapes, apricots, pears, or some other fruit into large sheets of fruit candy. I remember as a child when my grandmother Vartouhi used to make roejig and pastegh for my brothers and sister and me, which delighted us no end. She used to dry it in the sun on her back porch, making it the same way that she had as a young woman in Alabash many years before.

During the summer many fruits and vegetables were dried to be used throughout the winter months. Figs, dates, raisins, and apricots were the main fruits that were prepared in this way; and okra, string beans, and eggplants were some of the many vegetables that were dried, okra and stringbeans to be used primarily in soups and eggplant as a main ingredient in dolma. They also made tourshoo (pickles) from numerous vegetables, including green tomatoes, peppers, and string beans, and prepared their needed supply of tomato paste for the coming months. A staple in the Armenian diet is madzoon, so in the summer, madzoon was gotten from the villagers and dried and then put in bags for the winter.

They also prepared tarhana, which is a mixture of cooked wheat and dried madzoon, which they also bagged. These were but a few among many mainstay dishes that were prepared for the coming months. All of these foods were bagged and taken by her grandfather back to Marash, frequent trips being made by him throughout the summer, as the preparation of the foods was completed.

As busy as her grandfather was in the summer, he was still not too busy to spoil his oldest grandchild. Shnorhig was very picky in her eating habits, not liking raisins because of the seeds in them. So her grandfather used to pick small grapes with no seeds in them for her to eat throughout the summer. He also would dry these tiny grapes and make special raisins just for Shnorhig. In fact, he picked enough of the small grapes to make 20 to 25 pounds of tiny raisins so that they would be there for Shnorhig's grandmother to give her throughout the year as she wanted them. Another special way she remembers his pampering her was to remove the seeds from watermelon before giving it to her to eat, because she didn't like the seeds. So many little ways in their daily living to make her feel loved and special in the absence of her father.

All of this stopped suddenly during the night of April 24, 1915, when this little seven-year-old girl was awakened in the night by her grandfather, who told her that they must leave immediately on a journey. She did not yet understand what had happened, but many people in Marash, as well as other parts of Turkey, once Armenia, had already been brutally murdered. The Armenian Genocide had begun.

3

The Genocide and Death March

On that night in April of 1915 when my mother, little seven-year-old Shnorhig, left with her grandfather and most of the other members of her family on what was to become an incredibly long and painful journey, she could not imagine the years of suffering and heartbreaking loss that lay ahead. It was a long march — from Marash across Syria and Lebanon, to the Euphrates in Arabia (now Iraq). A very long march, if direct from point to point, but an even longer march because it was a zig-zag one, designed to exhaust the marchers so that they would collapse and die. So many did, either dying from exhaustion, starvation, disease, exposure, or beatings and other torture from the Turkish soldiers.

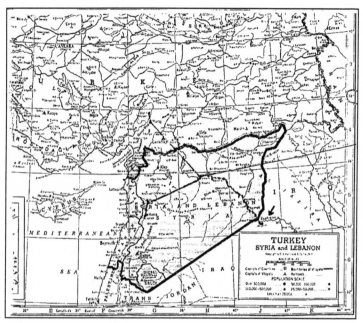

Map of Turkey, Syria, and Lebanon, showing the route of the Death March taken by Shnorhig and Vartouhi with the other members of their family as it would have been direct from point to point. But it was not that way, because the Turkish gendarmes made them walk in circles, covering the same territory numerous times before they moved forward. Thus, the zig-zag march from Marash to the Euphrates, and then to the refugee camps between Hama and Houmus in Arabia was so many times longer than a direct march would have been that it would be impossible to calculate the miles that they walked, though scholars of that period of history estimate about 1,000 miles.

Even after 80 years, the pictures of the cruelty and violence and brutal hardships they endured during those three years of marching and living in refugee camps are vivid in Shnorhig's memory today: "If you slowed down, the Turkish soldiers would beat you; if you stopped, they would beat you. They were constantly torturing you in horrible ways. They would select people to take away, which would create a commotion of screaming and crying. Those people were never seen again."

Of the population of those thousands of people on this death march, there were no young men to help and lead the others. It consisted of old people, children, and some young mothers with infants. Vartouhi, my grandmother, was one of the young mothers who was breastfeeding her nine-month-old son Barkev. Her milk stopped soon after the start of the exodus and she was unable to find anything that he could eat. Barkev was the first of our family of eighteen to die on the march.

Understandably, the youngest and the oldest died first on that march of horrors. That the eldest members of each community had been forced to leave their homes is incomprehensible, though none survived for long the horrendous conditions of that ordeal, as they died almost immediately. One such member of Shnorhig's family who did not leave on the Death March was her great-grandmother, her father's grandmother. She had died, fortunately, just prior to the start of the Genocide at age 105. Shnorhig has a vivid recollection of a very tiny, frail lady who was hard of hearing, dressed in a long quilted robe. Her mother had explained to her that she was dressed that way because she was very cold. She had been living for many years with one of her daughters who did expert tailoring, having her own sewing machine in her home and making the clothes for many of the members of the family.

Just prior to the start of the exodus, the Turks had struck the Armenians with a devastating blow. All of the Armenian educators, doctors, lawyers, writers, artists, and clergymen were brutally murdered. The Turks had forced Gomitas Vartabed, a great Armenian composer, musicologist, and a religious leader, to watch as seventy of the most elite of that group were tortured for days until they died. He couldn't bear it and lost his mind.

During that same period of time Turkish soldiers went through the cities rounding up all of the young Armenian men who had not yet been forced into the Turkish army and told their crying families that they were taking them elsewhere. In reality, they brutally murdered them that night. When their families went out in the morning, they saw the dead bodies of their loved ones either butchered or hanged. One of Shnorhig's uncles, Hagop Kerigian, was in a church praying when Turkish soldiers hanged him in the church, displaying his body the next morning in front of his home.

Another uncle was also being violently murdered at the same time in another part of the town. He was Vartouhi's younger brother, Setrag Kerigian, a 17-year-old student at the seminary, studying to be a priest. All of the windows and doors of the seminary were sealed by the Turkish soldiers, gasoline was poured inside, and the building was set ablaze. Turkish soldiers stood outside with guns in the event any of the young students might escape. Shnorhig's uncle and all of the other seminary students were burned alive.

Shnorhig's father was not present during this heinous period, as he was one of the young Armenian men who had been forced into the Turkish army four years before. Her memories of him are dim, but she remembers his coming home for a leave when she was six. Her recollection is a gathering at their home with their relatives and many friends there eating and talking. At the end, her father started hugging and kissing Shnorhig continuously and crying. Finally they separated them, Shnorhig staying at the top of the stairs and he at the bottom looking up at her. That is the last picture of her father that she has in her memory. And then he left, and she never saw him again.

Due to Shnorhig's grandfather's foresight and preparation for this horrendous journey, her family had an excellent supply of food in the beginning. A few days before the Genocide had begun, because of all of the visible tension and unrest in the region, her grandfather had taken all of their winter supplies of flour, chick peas, wheat, etc. to the miller to be ground into a nutritious mixed flour, which he had then taken to the baker to make into a thin, dry bread. It had been left in the oven at 150 degrees to dry it out, so that it could be kept for months without spoiling because there was no moisture in it. These thin breads were packed on the donkey that they had gotten for the journey, and this supply would have given them nourishment for many months had the Turkish gendarmes not beaten her grandfather and taken their donkey and the entire food supply from them within the first month of the journey.

One of the most poignant episodes in Shnorhig's mind was soon after that beating of her grandfather and the taking of their donkey and food supply. Villagers on the path of the march sometimes approached the Armenians with food that they wished to sell. Her grandfather still had a small amount of money that the Turkish soldiers had not been aware of, so he was able to buy squash, eggplant, and bulghour, enough for a small pan of dolma. Vartouhi prepared a small pan of it to put on the fire to cook. When the Turkish soldiers saw this, they came up to them and kicked the pan over and trampled on it. Vartouhi, bewildered, looked at them and asked, "Aren't you afraid of God? It has been months since we have had a decent meal, so why can't you give us a chance to have this?" When Shnorhig's grandfather spoke up in a similar way, the soldiers beat him unmercifully and then made them continue to march.

Another very vivid recollection is her grandfather's holding her and her little sister's hands as they walked because her mother always held her little baby brother in her arms. She still feels the pain of weeks that became grueling months and years of walking on the hot sands of the Arabian desert, her feet parched and bleeding from the rough pebbles on which she continuously stepped. Only once does she remember riding on a camel, in the beginning of the march when her grandfather had the money to rent one for a brief period, that too being a frightening experience. "Where are we going?" Shnorhig would repeatedly ask her grandfather, who would always answer with tears in his eyes, "Jerusalem, Jerusalem." In the past he had read her many Bible stories about Jerusalem, which she had imagined from the stories to be a very wonderful place. But it made no difference to her, as she would plead, "I don't want to go to Jerusalem! I want to go home!"

During those long, hard years of the Genocide, not only did Shnorhig and Vartouhi struggle each day to stay alive, but they had to live through, one by one, the deaths of the other members of the family, and then see their bodies carted away by the horse and wagon that picked up the dead each day and took them away to be thrown in a large hole. Some died during the march, and others died after they had arrived at their destination, which was Arabia. Shnorhig witnessed the deaths of her grandmother, her grandfather, her little sister and baby brother, two of her aunts, and the three children of one of her aunts and saw them all taken away. Vartouh witnessed all of the deaths until she was forced to leave her surviving family members in Arabia by Turkish soldiers.

In all of the family only her grandfather, who was a deeply religious man, had a funeral service. In the earlier part of the march when they had gotten to Syria, he told his daughter-in-law Vartouhi, "I know I cannot take this much longer; I am dying. If they come to you, even put a knife to your throat, do not give up your faith. It will only be for a few moments that you are in pain, but if you lose your faith, you will lose your life forever." That kind of powerful religious faith and devotion would be the guiding force in the lives of Vartouhi and Shnorhig, the only two members of our family who would ultimately survive the Genocide. Vartouhi performed his funeral service by reading from the Book of Timothy because as an ardent Christian he had asked her not to allow him to be put into the ground without a service.

Vartouhi did her best to shield Shnorhig from the most hideously cruel attacks on the marchers — Turkish soldiers viciously grabbing the girls and raping them on the road in front of their mothers, sisters, and brothers, ignoring their pleas and screams, feeling no shame or pity for their victims...or babies being violently cut out of the bellies of their mothers by the swords of the Turkish soldiers, leaving them both to die in their pool of blood on the side of the road.

Years later in America when mother and daughter talked of the Genocide, Vartouhi told Shnorhig that the worst sight that she personally had witnessed in the Genocide was of a mother's attempt to save her 14-year-old son's life. Because the boys were immediately killed at the start of the Genocide, the mother had dressed her son as a girl for the march. On the road, the Turkish soldiers, at one point, picked him as a girl to rape. When they took off his clothes and discovered that this was not a girl, they were enraged, screaming at the mother and beating her violently. Then they placed him so that his head was on her lap and chopped it off. She went completely wild, screaming uncontrollably until she died a few weeks later, his blood still on her. Those around her had begged her to wash it off as hoards of flies had been drawn to the blood, but she had refused because that was all that she had left of him.

During those terrible months of marching, they were living in the open spaces with no shelter of any kind. Finally, they arrived at a refugee camp in

Houmus in Arabia (Iraq). A sheik's wife, who had been left behind with a daughter, took pity on Vartouhi and Shnorhig and kept them in her home very briefly. Because my grandmother was an excellent cook and could prepare so many delicacies, Amooanna, the sheik's wife, benefited from having them with her as well. She was very kind to them and even saved their lives when a group of Arabs came into the camp in the night, as they would do a few times a year, taking girls and food and whatever else they could find and then leaving in the morning. During the raid the sheik's wife hid the two in her chicken coop and covered them with hay, Vartouhi keeping her hand on Shnorhig's mouth all night to keep her from making a sound. And so they were saved. For many years afterwards, my grandmother often mentioned Amooana to my mother, hoping that she was well and always praying for her because of her kindness to them.

Shnorhig's most painful memories of the march, however, concern her little sister Rosalia, who was only four years old when they left on the march. Because Vartouhi had her infant son to try to keep alive under those horrible conditions, Shnorhig always tried to help by taking care of Rosalia. As difficult as it was in the beginning, it was to become unbelievably horrendous for the two little sisters. After enduring many long months of pain and suffering on the march, their mother would be taken away from them during the period that they were in Arabia. They had been there for some months, and most of the other members of their family had already died or were very ill when Turkish soldiers, discovering that Vartouhi was a nurse, took her away from her two small daughters, forcing her to take care of Turkish soldiers in a nearby hospital. The emotional pain and agony of having to leave her children was horrible enough, but to be forced to take care of the soldiers who had not only killed most of her family members but also her husband was yet another form of torture that Vartouhi had to endure in silence. It was equally terrifying for Shnorhig, who was left alone to take care of herself and her little sister.

For Shnorhig that period in the Genocide is the most unbearably painful of all to remember. Eighty years later she still hears the continuous crying of her little sister, who was inconsolable. Day and night she tried to comfort her, but her tears never stopped. At night they slept in the open spaces or in doorways. Even today she wonders why the many rattlesnakes that were all around never bit them. By day she searched relentlessly to find something for them to eat — anything — a blade of grass or something from a garbage heap. Occasionally they were lucky to find edible flowers, the one that she remembers the best being the flower of the sweet pea. But mostly they survived on the grasses that she found, and she wonders how it was that none of the grasses that they ate were poisonous, as she did not know the difference.

The single most painful episode of the Genocide that is indelible in Shnorhig's memory is about Rosalia toward the end of her life. It was during a search for food that Shnorhig found half of a rotten lemon and was so excited about this find that she immediately took it to her little sister to eat. She could not get Rosalia to eat it, though she begged and begged her to do so. Rosalia just cried as she always did. Finally Shnorhig gave up trying to get her to eat it, and she ate it herself. Then she walked many miles to the hospital where Vartouhi was and begged them to let her mother come and help Rosalia, but they would not permit her even to see her mother. Soon after that her little sister died of starvation.

During the following long, horrible months, Shnorhig was alone, without even her little sister to sleep next to in open fields or in the doorways of others' homes, or to be a companion for whom she could search for some kind of food for the two of them to share. That horror of total aloneness for a little girl, herself in advanced stages of starvation, was overwhelming. When I asked her about it recently, she said: "Imagine what was going through my head as a small child — To have the memory of such a wonderful life before the Genocide and then to have watched it all taken from me. To lose my grandpa and grandma; to have my mother taken away from me to be a nurse in a Turkish hospital; to watch my baby brother die and later my blind aunt and my other aunt and her three children all slowly die in front of me; and, finally, worst of all, my baby sister, who I was closest to and loved so much. To watch her die. It was terrifying."

What she did was the only thing that they knew to do, and that was their relentless search for something to eat or drink. Each morning, she would say to herself, "Where can I look today? I went down that road yesterday and found nothing. Maybe I should go down this one today." The relentless search to find something to eat fortunately seemed to blot out the overwhelming emotional horror of what was actually happening to her and around her. Yet a vivid and powerful memory she still has that illustrates an emotional hurt from a child's perspective is one that she experienced in that period when she was alone. It concerned an instance when she was searching for water and something to eat, and some children in a house spotted her and called out to her, asking her if she wanted some water to drink. She responded that she did and approached the house. She got to the door and waited for them to open it and give her some water to drink, feeling very lucky about the offer. Suddenly, from the second floor, the children threw a bucket of water on her, laughing and cursing at her in a cruel way with ridiculing taunts. It shocked and startled her and, most of all, hurt her feelings so badly. They then came out and chased her, continuing to curse at her until they caught her and beat her. She has never forgotten that harsh cruelty she experienced as a frightened, lonely child, with no one to turn to for comfort or help or even just to express what had happened. Shnorhig lived with that kind of terrifying loneliness and feeling of abandonment for many long months.

After three long, horrible years, on November 11, 1918, the war ended. Vartouhi, released from the Turkish hospital, found Shnorhig who had miraculously survived the many months alone, and took her with fourteen orphans to an orphanage in Marash, where she herself had been put in 1895 when she had been orphaned during another Turkish rampage.

Their home in Marash was gone. Their family members were gone, all killed during those terrible three years past. Vartouhi said that once she went near the home where she had lived so happily with her family in Marash, the home that had belonged to her family but had been taken away from them by the Turks. And from a distance she saw the Turkish family that had claimed it and now lived in it, and she felt a very deep sadness and hurt for all of the enormous losses that they had experienced in the long three years past. Now it was only Vartouhi and Shnorhig. Vartouhi became a nurse at the hospital in Marash. She worked and lived there, near the orphanage where her only surviving child would be. She would keep a watchful eye over her frail daughter, and, with another nurse who was a friend of hers, they would try to nurse Shnorhig back to health, feeding her warm meat broth for many, many months because her insides were so dried out from starvation that she could not tolerate solid food.

4

Orphanage Life

Many of the children in the Marash orphanage were in advanced stages of starvation. Like Shnorhig, they were unable to tolerate solid food, as their insides had dried out from so many years of so little nourishment. They always had stomach-aches; many would vomit and be sick with fever. The matrons at the orphanage would boil meat or bones all day and give the broth to those children unable to tolerate solid food, hoping it would soften and lubricate their intestines enough so that the horrible effects of starvation could be reversed. This regimen of months of warm meat broth and silent prayers that it was not too late built up the resistance of some of the children so that they survived. But for many others it was too late.

Shnorhig remembers most of the children crying and constantly complaining of stomach pain. The matron and other staff members would console them and try to minimize what was happening. When their starvation was extremely advanced, those children were separated from the others and put in an infirmary-like place where they were given special care and attention. Most of those children were not seen again because they could not recover from the ravages of starvation and died. The staff tried to downplay what was happening so that the other children would not panic, as all of them were suffering from various stages of starvation. To have emphasized the deaths would have frightened the children even more than they already were.

The site of the orphanage in Marash where Shnorhig spent the next two years of her life was a large two-story building with running water. Though it was far from being as nice as living in one's home, it was, nevertheless, much more comfortable than many of the other facilities in that region of the world in those years that were suddenly transformed into orphanages. There were bathrooms, decent flooring, and mats to sleep on; and, as in most homes, there was a fireplace and hibachis for cooking as well as heating. The same method used in homes for creating warmth was used in the orphanages, too — that of a frame in the shape of a table with no top and a large blanket thrown on top of it with the hibachi centered underneath. Thirty to forty children could gather under it and warm their hands and feet, thereby warming their bodies before going to bed. Because there were so many children in the orphanage, the staff used it only in very cold weather for those children who were sick or coming down with a cold. Shnorhig remembers children saying, "I'm sick, I'm sick," hoping to get a chance to get the extra warmth of being under the blanket. The "Myrig", or mother figure, would check to see if the child had a fever and was really sick. Shnorhig says that she almost never got under the blanket, as she rarely got sick.

The orphanages were run by Protestant missionaries. However, they had a "Hyrig" (father) and a "Myrig" (mother) for each orphanage, Armenian men and women who tried both symbolically and functionally to be "parents" to the orphans. The Hyrig did the shopping, buying food and other necessary supplies. In the beginning of the Genocide, there were some funds for this, as contributions were arriving from various organizations and countries around the world. An example of this was while Shnorhig was in the Marash orphanage she remembers many boxes of old clothes and shoes arriving from America and the children trying on garments and shoes until they found something that fit them fairly well. As the years of horror continued, however, the contributions were fewer and fewer, so that later the orphanages were existing on almost nothing.

The Myrig of the orphanage did most of the cooking and tried to "mother" the children as much as one person could "mother" about 500 young children. The missionaries and all of the staff tried to help the orphans to keep their faith and hope, as did an Armenian minister, who also kept them aware of the Armenian religion and their heritage. There were also Armenian teachers who tried to teach the children to read and write in Armenian, but the children carefully hid their lessons whenever Turkish soldiers entered the orphanage, as they had been ordered to speak only in Turkish, never in the Armenian language, and certainly never to study anything about the Armenian religion and their heritage.

Just as food for the spirit could not be given freely or in abundance, so it was the same for food for the body. Somehow, the staff of the orphanage managed, whenever possible, to give the children two light meals a day, the breakfast being very skimpy. There was never a breakfast of eggs, as where would they have found 500 eggs so that each child could have an egg. A biscuit for each child was an impossibility as well, as that would have required almost 100 pounds of flour to make enough biscuits for all of the children in the orphanage. Instead, they gave them gravy to drink, made from five to ten pounds of flour and some meat broth and flavored with butter and onions. Each child at the orphanage had a small tin cup to eat and drink from. In that cup they had their gravy each morning, which not only filled them but warmed them as well. Then they were ready to do their chores.

Once in awhile Shnorhig remembers having a very special treat. This was so because Haroutoun, who was her cousin and three years older than she, would bring a pastry to the door of the orphanage and ask the Hyrig to give it to Shnorhig. He was selling them on the streets of Marash. His family who had been very well-off before the Genocide had lost their home and all of their possessions, so this was a way that he was trying to earn a little something for his mother and three younger brothers, because their father had already been killed by the Turks.

The main missionary of the Marash orphanage was a very kind Scottish woman named Miss Salmond. She used to call Shnorhig her granddaughter because Shnorhig's mother had also been under the guidance of Miss Salmond at the Marash orphanage years before when she had been orphaned after a violent Turkish outbreak. Although Miss Salmond had a very special affection for Shnorhig because of that connection, she also valued her because not only was she an exceptional student, but also very able in the recitation of poetry and other dramatic pieces.

The Protestant orphanages at that time had Biblical names, this one being named Beth Shalome. At Christmas all of the orphanages that were fairly closely situated to one another would come together for one celebration. There was always a program at these Christmas parties, and Shnorhig would represent her orphanage by reciting poetry. Years later she formed a close friendship with Vartanoush Berberian in Richmond, Virginia. Though they had never met as orphans because Vartanoush had been at a different orphanage, the name of hers being Ebeneezer, she, nevertheless, remembered Shnorhig because of her beautiful recitations at those Christmas parties.

Even their meager Christmas parties would soon become a distant memory, however, as the somewhat stable life of the orphans would once again be in turmoil. They would be forced to leave their orphanage at a moment's notice to points unknown. The journey would be frightening and perilous, as all matters connected with the Genocide had been.

There were events that led to this forced and hasty departure of the children in the orphanages in Turkey. The Turks had become enraged that the Armenians were pulling themselves together and surviving. Consequently, there was a new outbreak of violence by the Turks in 1920. All Armenians, at a moment's notice, were being put out of Marash, and all of Turkey for that matter, by the Turkish government. It was winter, and it would become another death march for many, as they would be unable to survive the severely cold weather and snow. It would force Vartouhi to make the most difficult decision of her life. She would have to leave Marash, as everyone was being forced out, but she knew that Shnorhig was still too frail and young to endure the long months of walking in the severe cold and snow. She felt that her daughter would have a greater chance for survival if she stayed within the context of the orphanage system, and so her only logical decision was not to take her daughter with her.

Shnorhig remembers her mother coming to the orphanage and putting a large white sweater on her that she had been crocheting the previous few months and also giving her a big bag of nuts and raisins, telling her daughter to eat one handful each day and not to take the sweater off until the warmth of spring had returned. Vartouhi assured her that she would come back for her, and then with enormous grief in her heart and with great courage she left her young daughter to go on a long, treacherous journey to an unknown destination.

Heartless as they were, the Turks also forced the orphans out of Turkey. The missionaries immediately took the children by foot to Haleb, Syria. It was a long, difficult, and painful journey. In Haleb they were piled into a train car for Beirut, Lebanon. From there they were transported by trucks to Shimlon, Lebanon, to another Protestant orphanage. This was a makeshift orphanage, as it was, in reality, a large storage building that had been converted into an orphanage. There was no special flooring; it was a dirt floor. There was no running water or a well at the orphanage, so they had to use the rain water

Shnorhig, at the right, with the children of the Hyrig and Myrig of the Shimlon Orphanage.

that accumulated in a big cement room. If that was low, they went to the village to get water from a spring or well, or they got water from a river that was a half hour away, the same river where the girls would bathe without soap, because there was none, and wash one another's hair with clay.

Looking at the Shimlon orphanage from the standpoint of its meagre physical conditions, perhaps a roof over their heads was the best that the orphans could hope for. Hundreds of young girls slept on skimpy mats on the dirt floor, which was the perfect setting for a nightmarish event that they all dreaded. Not infrequently during the night while asleep, girls were bitten by scorpions, the bite sometimes deadly, particularly if you were the unfortunate recipient of the first bite of the scorpion, which contained most of the poison. Once Shnorhig was bitten, but several girls had been bitten before her by the same scorpion, so very little poison got into her system and she survived the ordeal, though she still vividly remembers how terrifying it was.

The meagre aspect of orphanage life at Shimlon extended to other facets of their existence there, including education. As in the Marash orphanage, the children had schooling in this orphanage too, even though there were no pencils or paper or materials of any kind to be used in orphanages after the war. Instead, the children were always looking for pebbles and small rocks to use as their only classroom aid, using them to form letters and numbers. Even today, Shnorhig says that she is aware of small pebbles and rocks as she walks, as though she is still searching for them. Can you imagine learning to read and write in a language with no materials other than pebbles? Shnorhig did, and did it beautifully! In the two years in the Marash orphanage and the four years in the Shimlon orphanage, Shnorhig learned to master Armenian, as well as learn to speak Arabic and some French and a little English. She became well-versed in history, geography, the Armenian religion, and arithmetic as well. She no longer was forced to speak Turkish as they had been forced to do in the Marash orphanage and in the city of Marash. In fact, before the Genocide, the Armenians throughout Turkey had been forced not only to speak Turkish, but also to have Turkish names, her name being Lutfia and Vartouhi's name being Gulizar.

While the physical condition of the orphanage was not nearly as good as the orphanage in Marash, there were many positive features that greatly benefited them. The climate, for one, was a plus, as the weather was always warm, not requiring heating or shoes or warm clothing. If they did wear shoes, they were much like the wooden-sole clogs worn in America today. Because of the warm climate of Syria, there is an abundance of flowers and plants. Shnorhig remembers how very much she and the other orphans enjoyed the chewing gum that came from one of the plants. They would put a leaf on a rock that had been cleaned, break open the leaf, and then allow the liquid to drip onto the rock. It would dry and become delicious gum, much to their delight! They also used to love to gather pine cones, because from each of the cones they were able to remove as many as a dozen pine nuts, which they greatly enjoyed eating.

Shnorhig has some very special memories of the Shimlon orphanage. It was during her life there that she had a small garden of her own. The girls in the middle age group (12 to 14) were given a little plot of land which was 4 feet by 4 feet to grow a type of flower. Hers was snapdragons. It meant a great deal to her to tend her little garden of snapdragons and watch them flourish. Seventy-five years later at her 85th birthday party hosted by my brother Yervant at the 2300 club in Richmond,

Virginia, the room was full of snapdragons. Eighty-some people were there with her in celebration.

Another very wonderful memory of that period spent in the Shimlon orphanage concerned a gift from children in America who had brought offerings to their Sunday schools for the orphans abroad. Some of that money had been used to buy bolts of different colored ribbon which were sent to various orphanages, one of them being the one in Shimlon. The matron of the orphanage selected a color for each age group; perhaps green for the oldest girls, purple for the next, etc. She remembers how thrilled all of them were to have their hair pulled back with a bright-colored ribbon, that it brightened the drabness of the orphanage seeing that little touch of color on the hundreds of young girls who were there.

Though the children in the Shimlon orphanage had such a meagre existence, there was, nevertheless, a thoughtful generosity of spirit in them that is rather remarkable. While in this particular orphanage for four years, Shnorhig remembers that once a week they went without their meal for that day in order to send the amount of money it would have cost for that meal to the starving children in China or elsewhere in the world. The meal would not have necessarily been large; perhaps it would have only been a piece of bread and a few olives. But when all of the children gave that up, a small amount of money could be sent to those children elsewhere in the world who were starving. She remembers that she and the other children never felt resentment for losing their meal, which they indeed greatly needed themselves. On the contrary, she remembers how they would pray all day for the starving children in China.

The question of food brings up the most positive feature of the Shimlon orphanage — its location. Since Shimlon was in the country, there were farmers all around them, many who would bring leftover crops that they could spare and leave them for the orphans. They would leave tomatoes, yellow squash, zucchini, long cucumbers, and watermelons, to name a few, and whatever else they had by season.

The food that they left was wonderful and generous, but not enough to feed all of the nearly 500 children there, so a system was created where the orphans worked for their food by helping the farmers in the fields. They would rise early, go in a large group to the fields, and harvest the crops that were ready. At noon they had a good meal: perhaps pilaf made with bulghour and certainly some of the vegetables and fruits that they had just picked; they usually drank tine (madzoon in water). Then they would rest for a few hours in the fields, later resuming their work until dusk. Shnorhig remembers it as being fun, the comraderie of working together. After all, they were a big "family": the children playful and loving with each other, and the Hyrig and Myrig of the orphanage their "parents".

Orphanage life, however, as Shnorhig experienced it for the six years that she lived in two orphanages, was a very disciplined environment, as the matron could be very strict, and there were always many chores for all of the children to do, with no accompanying frills. So the orphans created, in a sense, little family units, for much-needed warmth and nurturing, much the way sisters, aunts, and other relatives might function with one another.

Because there were so many girls at both orphanage sites where Shnorhig lived, they were frequently recognized by numbers, rather than by their names, Shnorhig's number being 235 in the Shimlon orphanage. Number 235 was an excellent student, ranking first in her class academically. She did not realize that a scholarship fund had been started for her by Miss Salmond after she had retired and returned to her home in Scotland. Each month

*Shnorhig (center, bottom row) with classmates at the Shimlon orphanage.
She was the youngest in her class.*

Miss Salmond sent money to be put in the fund so that Shnorhig would have a scholarship to Beirut University when she reached the age for college.

Miss Frierson, a Protestant missionary also from Scotland and head of the Shimlon orphanage, called her in to tell her of the scholarship that had been created for her by Miss Salmond. She agreed with Miss Salmond's choice, as she too ranked Shnorhig as the top student in her class scholastically. Shnorhig was excited about this honor they wished to bestow on her, though she would never be able to accept it because her life would take a different turn.

The only other member of her family, her mother, had also survived the Genocide, though Shnorhig did not know this. In the beginning of their separation, Shnorhig had cried continuously, asking the matron when her mother would return for her. But as the months passed, she had given up the intense waiting and resigned herself to the unknown. Miraculously, Vartouhi had survived the hardships of the long, torturous march out of Marash in the winter of 1920, though half of the people on the march had died before they had finally found refuge in Cyprus. Vartouhi had come to America in 1921, and months later she had met and

Vartouhi with friends from Marash and Cyprus. She is on the front row, second from the left.

Vartouhi's wedding picture of her second marriage, including Zadoor Soghoian on the right, her second husband's cousin.

Vartouhi and Ghazaros and their infant son Vartan. This picture was sent to the Shimlon orphanage as a way to identify Vartouhi to Shnorhig.

married a fine Armenian man who had also lost his family in the Genocide. She cried constantly, however, not really able to begin a new life because of the grief in her heart for her lost daughter Shnorhig, wondering what had happened to her first-born. Was she alive? Had she survived? And if so, where was she? Vartouhi continuously agonized over these unanswered questions, and with the help of her caring husband Ghazaros Soghoian, they searched throughout the Middle East by placing ads in the Lost and Found sections of the newspaper in that region until they got the answer that they were praying for — Shnorhig was alive! Because Vartouhi was not yet an American citizen, it would take many long months before they would finally be able to complete the arrangements for their reunion in America.

At age sixteen, nine years after the start of the Genocide, the arrangements were finally completed for her release to her mother, and Shnorhig left Beirut on a French cargo ship, the Federal Line Praga, travelling third class. She left for America and the start of a new life, reuniting with her mother for the last time.

5

The Journey to a New World

Embarking on her long journey to America, Shnorhig boarded the Praga on May 1, 1924, arriving in Providence, Rhode Island, on May 31. She would have many new experiences, some wonderful and some not, on this long voyage at sea. But soon after the start of her voyage, something happened to transform this seemingly unpleasant journey into a positive adventure. Possibly because she was a young girl travelling alone, the ship's nurse selected her to be the baby sitter for the children of a young missionary couple returning to the United States for a visit. They were kind and generous people who made arrangements for Shnorhig to eat with them in First Class and remain with them throughout the day, only sleeping in her own quarters at night.

This arrangement came about after the first stop of the ship, which was Damascus, where the Nelsons, who were missionaries from there, boarded. Because it was a cargo ship, oranges were being left in Damascus and other goods being put aboard the ship for the next port. When she began to babysit for the Nelsons, her English greatly improved. They had a map and showed her the location of each port that they went to, explaining, as well, what goods would be taken to that port and what goods would be picked up. They also gave her a little geography and history lesson about each city and region where they were docked.

During her 30 days at sea, not only did her English improve enormously, but so did her French. Each morning of the trip, the French nurse would come down with hot tea for her, comb her hair and help her get ready, and then take her upstairs to the Nelsons where she would have breakfast with them. At each port the couple would leave the ship to sightsee, and Shnorhig would take care of their two children, 9-month-old Oscar and 2½-year-old Jane. They always returned with little gifts for her, such as ribbons for her hair and bracelets and combs, so that by the end of the trip she had acquired a bag full of little treasures. She remembers when they went to Romania, they brought her a necklace and a bracelet, which she liked very much. After being an orphan for so many years and being denied the pretty things a young girl wants and enjoys, that gift was very special to her.

By the time Shnorhig got to Providence, Rhode Island, she had lost lots of weight, because she had been seasick most of the time on the long voyage. Yet she had gained so much too, especially her ability to speak English, so much improved now, as well as her knowledge of the geography of the regions travelled. In fact, her first "official" encounter on United States soil impressed her so much that she still remembers it with pride today. It concerned a United States inspector in the Immigration Office of the Port of Entry at Providence, Rhode Island, from whom she had to take an oath. He asked her many questions about herself — her past experiences, her trip to America, and her goals and hopes for the future. The inspector was so impressed by her ability to understand his questions and by the answers that she gave that he patted her on the shoulder and told her that he was sure that she would have a wonderful future in America.

Her arrival in this wonderful new land had confirmed this excited sixteen-year-old's high expectations for her new life in America. But it was going to get even better. Mr. Nelson took her with his family to the home of his brother, a dentist in Providence. He owned a big, beautiful three-story house where Shnorhig was given her own bedroom with a beautiful canopy bed. She had her own bathroom as well! These were incredible firsts, as was her first experience with electric lights and a maid serving her all kinds of new and unusual foods. Fondly she remembers putting sugar on her eggs to the amusement of the maid! In the Old Country she had never seen spoon sugar, so she thought that she was using salt.

For two wonderful nights she stayed there with the Nelsons and enjoyed it immensely. Then they took her to New York City for the two most memorable days of sightseeing that she could have ever imagined! There were more wonderful gifts, including chocolates! Her most exciting and awe-inspiring memory, however, is seeing Grand Central Station in all its majesty. There the Nelsons, who had made her feel so welcome and special, put

Horakour, the senior member of the Kerigian family, surrounded by Vartouhi and Ghazaros and their infant sons Vartan and Avedis and daughter Shnorhig, and Santookht and Siervart Kerigian, soon after the sisters and Shnorhig had arrived in America.

her on a train to Binghampton, New York, but not before buying her more chocolates and other candies and the latest ladies' magazines from the many barkers who were selling their wares at the doors of the departing trains. Shnorhig's destination was

Binghampton, New York, because awaiting her there were her mother, her stepfather Ghazaros, and her two infant brothers, two-year-old Vartan and one-year-old Avedis. To make sure that Shnorhig did not fall into the hands of the wrong people, the Nelsons had made arrangements for a travel agent to meet her at the train station to help her find her mother.

My mother has a very special place in her heart for the Fourth of July, because that is the day that she and her mother were finally reunited after so many long and painful years of separation — reunited in their new country. She soon discovered that the train station was packed with Armenians, as they had all come there with her mother and family to welcome Shnorhig and congratulate Vartouhi on their long-awaited reunion.

The reunion of mother and daughter was almost overwhelming. There were so many Armenians, excited and talking, and approaching her. Then she saw a woman who favored her mother coming toward her. From 1920 to 1924, they had been lost from one another. In 1920 Shnorhig had come up to her mother's chin; now in 1924, this woman who might be her mother, came up to her shoulder! "You look familiar, but you're not as beautiful as my mother. And you're so short!" Shnorhig uttered in confusion.

Vartouhi, who was run-down and sick from the horrible years of the Genocide and now having two infant sons, looked at her daughter with understanding and love in her eyes. "Dear one," she explained, "I have not gotten smaller. You have grown up. Oh, Lutfia!"

Her daughter looked deeply into her mother's eyes, knowing that she had finally found her, and answered, "Don't ever call me that again, Mother. My name is Shnorhig."

6

Early Life in America

After having spent four painful years of separation from one another, the reunion of mother and daughter was full of emotion. Dozens of happy Armenians surrounded them, also trying to welcome this young Armenian girl with their embraces and warm words of affection. Cries of congratulations to her mother and stepfather began to be almost overwhelming, so that Shnorhig was glad when they began to make their way home, away from all the noise of her homecoming.

When they finally got to her mother's home in America, Shnorhig was truly shocked. It was a small, third-story apartment in a poor section of Binghampton. Their small apartment at 99 Clinton Street not only had no electricity, but there was only one gaslight in the hall; the rest of the apartment had oil lamps. She also soon discovered that there was no hot water in their apartment. To bathe, her mother had to heat water in the kitchen and take a large pan of it to the bathroom, which Shnorhig mixed with cold water. She was truly disappointed because she had heard in the orphanage that in America there was hot running water and a cord which could be pulled that produced light. This was not the America that she had been told about! The America she had been told about was the America that she had found in Providence — where there was hot and cold running water, her own bath, and her own beautiful bedroom with canopy bed. In a few short days she had come to a small third floor apartment at 99 Clinton Street where there was no faucet from which hot water came, no electric lights, no beautiful canopy bed. Instead, there was the constant smell of gasoline from the gas station behind their small apartment, making her feel sick and nauseated. Everything was so foreign and different for the young girl who had been apart from her mother for such a long time, the mother she had been denied during their long years of separation and her difficult and lonely years of growing up in orphanages.

A few days later her mother found her young daughter crying softly in a corner. Very concerned, she asked, "Are you sick? What is wrong? Why are you crying?" In her few short days in America, Shnorhig had already tasted both sides of America, and it was a shock to her. Confused, she spoke to her mother from her heart, telling her about the sick feeling she was having from the smell of the gasoline and that the way that they were living was not the way America was supposed to be. The way it had been in Providence was America.

Vartouhi answered her unhappy daughter with great wisdom: "There are two Americas; one is like this, and one is like the America you found in Providence. I hope with all my heart that someday you will have that America."

And "have that America" she did ultimately, though there would still be many more painful hurdles and struggles to overcome in her new life before arriving there.

The most immediate one was the matter of schooling. Because of her limited English, the administrators at the Daniel Dickinson School put her in fourth grade even though she was sixteen. The children in her class were cruel, laughing at her because of her size and limited English. The teachers and administrators felt sorry for her and moved her into fifth grade, but the situation was the same, as those children were, at the most, eleven years old — too young to understand, but old enough to be cruel and hurt her feelings too. Even in such a hostile environment, she was a quick learner, soaking up much information in the one year that she attended public school. She remembers learning the names of the then-48 states and their capitals as well as other pertinent data about each state. Also, one non-academic experience that she had when attending public school she still fondly remembers. The children in her class were taught to make Jell-O™, much to Shnorhig's delight. She showed her mother the Jell-O™ packages in the grocery store, and they bought two of them, which she prepared that same evening. Her mother and stepfather thought it was wonderful and praised her, making her feel very excited and happy about her accomplishment.

Throughout the year that she attended Daniel Dickinson School, her teachers praised her for being such an excellent student, but after one year she felt that it was time to leave day school, as she couldn't really fit in with the children in the classroom or on the school yard. She then attended continuation school all day on Thursdays and worked during the other days at the shoe factory where her stepfather worked. However, she had learned enough English to function as a translator when a teacher would come two afternoons a week to her mother's apartment to teach citizenship to the Armenian ladies in that apartment building and neighborhood. Shnorhig loved helping in that way, just as she loved taking care of her two baby brothers whom she adored. Her formal schooling would stop when she married one year later at age 18, though she has never stopped learning, throughout her life being an avid reader in both Armenian and English.

But we must not speak of her marriage at 18 until we get her engaged! That happened rather quickly; on August 14, 1927, Shnorhig Keshishian became engaged to Zadoor Soghoian. In the two years that she had lived in America, she had met other young Armenians at the social gatherings that were held in their community. In fact, her stepfather had taken her to the finest department store in Binghampton to buy her a beautiful dress to wear to those gatherings, as he was very proud of the poetry recitations that she gave in the programs. This kind, thoughtful man had spent one week's paycheck, which was sixteen dollars, to buy his

Shnorhig and Zadoor's engagement picture with Vartouhi and Ghazaros and their two children, Vartan and Avedis.

stepdaughter her beautiful dress. Many young men had approached him for her hand in marriage, but it was not until she met Zadoor that she wanted to say "yes."

Zadoor was her stepfather Ghazaros Soghoian's cousin. They had lost their family in the Genocide, both of them having come to America before 1915. When the Genocide had begun, Zadoor had wanted to return to his home in Turkey to try and help the Armenians, but Ghazaros had refused to sign for him, as he was underage, saying that he could not risk losing him too.

Zadoor, who had travelled and worked in other parts of the United States, had come to Binghampton for a visit from Virginia, where he had been living with his older brother Bedros, his only relative in America other than Ghazaros and a truly delightful individual with whom he had a close bond. As soon as Zadoor met Shnorhig, he knew immediately that she was the beautiful young girl that he wanted to marry, and he commenced to sweep her off her feet.

There was very little courtship in the Armenian community in those days, and so any "dating" that was done was chaperoned. This is not to say that my father's courtship of my mother was run-of-the-

Shnorhig and Zadoor Soghoian's wedding picture.

mill. On the contrary. When he came to visit her, for example, he did not bring her a one-pound box of sugared almonds; it was a five-pound box! On one of the few dates that they had at a movie theater — chaperoned of course — Zadoor asked Shnorhig if she would like some popcorn. When she answered "yes," he bought her all of the popcorn in the machine! An engagement was imminent! Taking her to a fine department store to buy her an engagement dress, Zadoor liked all five dresses that she tried on, so he bought her all five!

On October 9, 1927, two months after their engagement, Shnorhig and Zadoor were married in a beautiful wedding ceremony. She looked radiant in her lovely gown, and he was handsome in his wedding suit. The suit had been a gift from a tailor for whom he had performed a service, renovating his shop into two places of business by building a partition for him. Zadoor was a talented man who could fix almost anything, finding time throughout his life to help people solve various types of problems.

Having lost so much at age seven, Shnorhig would finally have a chance to make up for it. After her beautiful wedding and first year of marriage, Shnorhig and Zadoor were thrilled when they had their first child, my oldest brother Marshall. A cloud came over their joy, however, when they lost their second child the following year, one week after his birth with heart problems. But enormous joy returned to them with my brother Yervant's birth the following year, followed by my sister Rose's arrival, and eventually my birth and my brother Richard's.

"Have that America" she did. Shnorhig's bounties lay ahead, starting first at age eighteen with meeting and marrying Zadoor Soghoian, the finest of men with the same strength of character and moral convictions that she possessed. Together they created a life of service and commitment to their fellow human beings and raised five children who have followed in their footsteps.

Shmorhig and Zadoor's group wedding picture, including also Vartouhi and Ghazaros's two sons and Nishan and Mayrie's three children and Nishan's younger brother Hovannes, who came to America after Vartouhi's cousin in Cyprus had made the arrangements for him to do so.

Shnorhig and Zadoor Soghoian in their wedding picture with their best man and matron of honor, Nishan and Mayrie Kerneklian. Nishan was the soldier who went on the Marash-Cyprus march with Vartouhi and later they came to America as "brother" and "sister." Mayrie was one of the orphans in the Cyprus orphanage that Vartouhi brought to America.

Another photograph of Shnorhig and Zadoor on their wedding day.

Shnorhig and Zadoor's three oldest children: Rose, Marshall, and Yervant as preschoolers.

7

Circles of Love

Circles of love were born out of the struggle to survive the horrors of the Genocide. They would create everlasting bonds of devotion and commitment that would never be broken. And after the Genocide, survivors came together to form new patterns of friendship and love in a new land — much the way the intricate patterns of Vartouhi's Armenian needle lace and Shnorhig's crocheted pieces were being formed — appearing delicate and fragile, but in reality very durable and lasting.

Some of these deep bonds of commitment had their genesis in horrible moments of the Genocide. One such time was the long, perilous journey of many Armenians forced from Marash by the Turks during the winter of 1920, of which Vartouhi was a part. As a nurse, she had helped many survive the march through her medical aid and spiritual counsel, and in the process formed deep friendships that would remain until her death. One example were three well-educated sisters who were on the march with their elderly mother, who became ill from the hardships of the journey and unable to walk in the snow. Nishan Kerneklian, a young Armenian soldier with the French Foreign Legion that Vartouhi had nursed in the hospital in Marash, carried this elderly lady on his back for many miles until she was able to walk again. She and her daughters survived the march and came to America, settling in the Boston area, where Vartouhi visited them many times, their close friendship remaining throughout their lives. One sister was Santootht, a music teacher, and another was Arousiag, a nurse, who later married a Yale graduate, who also was Armenian.

During that march from Marash, a tragedy occurred involving Vartouhi's sister-in-law and her four children. Her husband and Hovannes, Vartouhi's husband, had been brothers, and both had already died in the Genocide. Now her two youngest sons, Bedros and Bogos, would also perish, freezing to death on the journey, the harshness of the winter too much for their young bodies to withstand. Only she and her two oldest sons, Haroutoun and Garabed Keshishian, would survive that terrible winter ordeal. The two youngest had been Shnorhig's age, which heightened the wisdom of Vartouhi to have left her young and frail daughter behind. Later the two surviving sons settled in South America with their mother; each had five children, as did Shnorhig. They corresponded regularly with my grandmother and mother and spoke by phone with them throughout their lives, though they were never able to see each other again.

Another miraculous survivor of the Genocide who settled in South America was the son of Hagop Kerigian, Vartouhi's cousin. At the start of the Genocide, Hagop is the relative who had been praying inside a church in Marash when Turkish soldiers had come in and hanged him, then taking his body from the church and displaying it the following morning in front of his home. At the time, his wife was pregnant with their only child, who somehow was born in all of that violence and bloodshed and survived the Genocide, later moving to South America and getting his Ph.D.

After the Marash-Cyprus march, Vartouhi did much good in the months that she was in Cyprus before coming to America. She had a cousin in

Cyprus, a minister who ran an orphanage for boys. Through him, she became a matron at an orphanage for girls, helping them cope with their shattered, disrupted lives, as well as giving them hope for the future. Two of the girls that she helped in the orphanage, Santootht and Siervart Kerigian, were relatives from her mother's side. Their mother who lived near the orphanage was widowed and had no means to care for them, and so they were living in the orphanage.

After months of being in Cyprus, Vartouhi and the young soldier Nishan Kerneklian decided to come to America, as both had lost their families and yearned for a new beginning. They vowed to be as brother and sister for the rest of their lives, which they honored to their deaths. At the time of their departure, Nishan's younger brother, Hovannes Kerneklian, was in the orphanage of Vartouhi's cousin. This kind minister completed the necessary papers and made all of the arrangements for Hovannes to come to America to join his brother Nishan, but the minister himself never made that journey. With his wife and four children, all of whom were well-educated, they chose to remain in Cyprus.

Even though Vartouhi had come to America and within six months had married again, she had

The Cyprus orphanage staff, including Vartouhi, second row, third from the left.

been unable to start a new life because her heart was aching with unanswered questions about her lost daughter Shnorhig. When she miraculously found her alive, during those long months of finalizing the arrangements for their reunion in America, she was continuing to help other Armenian orphan girls, hoping to make it possible for them to begin new lives in America, too.

Santookht and Siervart Kerigian, the two sisters who had been in the Cyprus orphanage with her and also her relatives, were among those that she helped. Through her efforts, they were able to come to America with their mother. The Kerigian sisters met Shnorhig in New York soon after all three had arrived there, and they became as close as sisters could be, remaining that way throughout their lives. All of them married Armenian men and had children. Over the years Santookht and her husband Dan Akullian often visited Vartouhi and Shnorhig and their families in Virginia. Santootht died a few years ago, but Siervart Alexanian and Shnorhig have continued their close friendship, meeting in the Boston area where Siervart lives, as well as having brief reunions in Rhode Island and Connecticut in the last five years. While they have always communicated by letter or phone, even

Shnorhig Keshishian (left) with Santookht (center) and Siervart Kerigian when all three had newly arrived in America and become friends.

their advanced years have not kept them from visits together.

Other orphans that Vartouhi helped at that time were the five oldest girls in the Cyprus orphanage, making arrangements for them to leave orphanage life and come to America for a new beginning. All of them married young Armenian men in Binghampton, New York, where Vartouhi was living with her husband Ghazaros. In fact, one of the girls Mayrie married Nishan Kerneklian. The two families have remained close for the last 70 years, though Vartouhi, Nishan, and Mayrie are now dead. Particularly close to Shnorhig and her family is Nishan's oldest daughter, Berjoohi Street, and her husband and children.

All of the young girls from the orphanage that Vartouhi and her husband were instrumental in bringing to America remained indebted to them for the rest of their lives. The link of the orphanage connection indeed deep, others also did not forget Vartouhi's attempts to help them when they had been orphaned during the Genocide. Two of those orphans were Yeghsapet and Martha Akullian, two sisters who were among the fourteen children that Vartouhi had gathered together in 1918 after the initial violence of the Genocide had subsided for a brief

Shnorhig with her two baby brothers in America.

period, in order to take them back to Marash with her daughter Shnorhig. She had looked for orphaned children from the region of Marash in order to return them to their home area, with the hope that other family members had survived too and that they would find each other. The two Akullian sisters had been put into the Marash orphanage with Shnorhig. Years later in America, they found Vartouhi, and with their families came to see her to personally thank her for her help in saving their lives, remaining life-long friends with Vartouhi and Shnorhig.

Bringing with them the hurts and horrors of the past to a present filled with hopes and dreams, new circles of love and devotion were being formed in their new world of America, too. One such example was at 99 Clinton Street in Binghampton, New York, where Vartouhi and Ghazaros lived with their two infant sons, Vartan and Avedis, and 16-year-old Shnorhig on the third floor. Piloon Manoogian lived on the second floor with her parents, and the Abashian family lived on the first floor. Piloon and Shnorhig were about the same age and became the closest of friends, remaining that way to the present time. Piloon later married Arthur Najarian, and the Soghoian children and the Najarian children have been as close to each other throughout their lives as

Shnorhig and Avedis, her only surviving brother, who retired from the Marine Corps.

relatives could be. Laura, one of the Abashian children says that her earliest memories as a preschooler is playing on the front steps with a brown-eyed, dark-haired little boy. Twenty years later she met him again and they fell in love and married, ready to celebrate their 50th wedding anniversary this year. That little boy was Avedis Soghoian, Shnorhig's little baby brother!

The Armenian families living at 99 Clinton were very close to each other in many ways, enjoying socializing together and, more importantly, always helping one another in any way that they could. One example of that kind of closeness and caring came about when one of the Abashian children, infant Steve, became ill. He was not improving, and naturally his mother became alarmed. When Vartouhi saw him, she knew that he needed immediate medical attention. She remained calm and told her dear friend Escoohi to watch all of their children, and she, in her robe and slippers, grabbed the sick baby and literally ran to the hospital where he got the medical attention he needed and recovered from the illness.

At the center of this evolving circle of love and respect was the senior member of our family, Gadar Kerigian. All of us called her Horakour, which means sister of your father, because Vartouhi's father and Horakour had been sister and brother. Before the start of the Genocide, Horakour and her husband and two small children had left for America. But a tragic fate had befallen her when her husband and one of her children had become ill on the voyage, dying soon after they had arrived in New York. Although Horakour had a college degree from the American University in Marash, she was never able to get comparable work in the Bronx in New York City, where she raised her only surviving child alone and lived for most of her life. Being Shnorhig's great-aunt and Santootht and Siervart's great-aunt as well, the children of all of these families looked up to Horakour as a very special lady, which indeed she was, treating her with enormous respect until her life ended, when she had almost reached the century mark.

Just as Horakour had come to America before the Genocide, my father, Zadoor Soghoian, had also done so. His father had sent him from their home in Kharpert, a region in Turkey, when he was only 15, because he didn't want his son to be forced into the Turkish army when he was of age. At the start of the Genocide in 1915, he had wanted very much to go back and help his family, but had been unable to return. Consequently, he devoted the rest of his life to helping every Armenian that he met who needed assistance of any kind, be it financial, work-related, or of a personal nature. He was enormously generous in helping not only individual Armenians, but groups as well. One instance was over sixty years ago when he was a young married man with several small children. Even with all of those responsibilities, he sent $250, which was a sizable amount of money in those years, to Armenia for a special piece of equipment much needed in a Myranoush, a birthing place.

I remember he and my mother helping so many Armenians in numerous ways throughout their lives. They were among a handful of families in Richmond, Virginia, who worked diligently and steadfastly to make the creation of an Armenian church in their community a reality. My father was one of the Godfathers of St. James Armenian Church in Richmond, Virginia, when it was consecrated forty years ago, and throughout his life he faithfully worked in church activities. My mother was Chairlady of the Ladies' Auxiliary for eighteen years out of the first thirty years of the Armenian Church in Richmond; she was on the executive board most of the other years. Also very active in

Shnorhig with other Armenian ladies in the kitchen of St. James Armenian Church, in Richmond, Virginia, preparing food for the Church Bazaar. From L to R: Anna DerKrikorian, Satenig Garabedian, Shnorhig Soghoian, and Marguerite Koustigian.

civic affairs, through her joint efforts with Dr. Jack Garian and Dr. George Vranian, they made it possible for the Armenian Church to participate in the Virginia State Fair for many years. Likewise, she worked with Harry Tatian in involving our church's participation in the Boys' Club International Food Festival, which has been a very important yearly event in Richmond for 25 years.

Another much-attended food festival in Richmond, started soon after the Armenian Church was consecrated, was the Bazaar and Food Festival of St. James Armenian Church. Done annually, Shnorhig's Co-Chairlady for the first one was Yeghsapet Baronian. Many years before when Shnorhig had been in the Shimlon orphanage, Yeghsapet's mother, Nazenguil Bektermerian, had sewn the clothes for the children in that orphanage. Though they had not personally known one another at the time, years later when their paths crossed again in the new world, Shnorhig became friends with this very sweet lady and her daughter. Mrs. Bektermerian reached out to Shnorhig, a young, busy mother of five small children, even offering to sew curtains and slipcovers for her if she needed them. Though Shnorhig never accepted her generous offer, she valued her for her thoughtfulness and friendship.

But most of all, she made the lives of so many elderly Armenian ladies in Richmond, who have all passed on now, happier and more fulfilling because of her sensitivity to the painful memories of horror that they carried in their minds and souls from the atrocities of the Genocide. They had all been older than she, many of them having been brutally attacked by Turkish soldiers and their children killed in front of them. None had had the good fortune of learning to read and write in Armenian or English. So my mother gave of herself, treating each of them in the most loving and special way, making every meeting, luncheon, and dinner that they had at the Church a special time for them. And most of all, being a true friend to each one of them, creating circles of love that would be nourishing for each and that would never be broken.

8

Giving Back in the New World

Two courageous women, Shnorhig and Vartouhi, from the very beginning embraced their new
country with love, giving unselfishly not only to
their families and friends, but also to the countless
people they met in life who were ill and hurting and
in need. There are so many instances that I could
relate, but will limit my examples to but a few.

Vartouhi lived most of her life in America in
the small town of Hopewell, Virginia, where it
became necessary for her to operate their grocery
store after her husband became very ill almost 20
years after their marriage and lay bedridden
upstairs where they lived. She still found time then
and throughout her life to help those who were ill
and in need. In the back of their store she had

cultivated the most exquisite little rose garden which was about eight feet square. Everyone who saw it was ecstatic over the beauty of her roses, many wanting to buy them, which they did frequently. That money she kept in a large coffee can, using it for those in the community who were ill. When visiting an ill woman, she took her two large cans of juice and a gown; for a man she took juice and pajamas. Always with her gifts were her prayers and her healing manner.

She touched the lives of so many people in this way, though the example I remember the best was a young girl about seven who lived in a small house across the field behind her store. Her mother was dying of cancer, and the child was left to take care of herself. My grandmother brought her home one day, stuck her in the tub and gave her a bath, washed her clothes, put her in bed to nap, fed her a good meal in her clean clothes, and then sent her home. She took care of that child in that way for about a year, until her mother died and relatives took the daughter away to live with them.

Years later my mother was in a restaurant with friends in Richmond, Virginia, when a young woman sitting at a nearby table kept staring at her. She soon approached my mother and confirmed her belief that she was "Mrs. Kaiser's" daughter (as my grandmother had been known by many in Hopewell). She told everyone at the table how she had so often thought of that wonderful woman who so many years before had helped her when she had needed it and had given her hope to go on. She was happily married now with a daughter about the same age as she had been many years before when Mrs. Kaiser had been so kind to her.

Vartouhi not only helped so many people in her own community, but her concern and help extended to all parts of the world. While she was never financially wealthy, she somehow, throughout her life in America, found ways to keep small amounts of money aside in order to send checks each year to missionaries around the world helping those less fortunate. When she, her daughter, and others close to her had needed help, missionaries had helped them; she never forgot that. So she in turn did her best to assist them in helping others.

Like her mother before her, my mother has also spent her life trying to comfort those in need and in pain. She has been enormously generous in sharing her talents and abilities with others to make their lives more comfortable, more beautiful, and more fulfilling. I could write volumes about her good deeds and generosity of spirit, but, as in the case of my grandmother, I will only give you a few examples of her remarkable ability to be truly giving and caring.

As far back as my childhood I remember my mother visiting those who were ill. One particular situation comes immediately to mind because it was so constant and long-term. Mother knew a much older woman who, bedridden at home, was dying of cancer. It was a fairly long walk to her home, but almost every evening we walked there, usually with some kind of food. Mother would sit by her bed and talk with her while my little brother and I would play quietly in another room. My sister, who is a little older, would often go with us, bringing her books in order to do her homework while we waited for mother. This went on for months and was very tiring for us, but Mother continued her bedside vigil until the woman's death.

Many shut-ins that we knew in the community would not accept visitors, but made an exception for my mother because she made them feel better and gave them hope, and they felt at ease with her quiet, gentle manner. Often she took one of many Armenian dishes she so expertly prepares: dolma (stuffed vegetables with meat and rice), cheoregs (an Armenian bread), yahlanchi (grape leaves and rice), tourshoo (Armenian pickles made from many vegetables), madzoon (yogurt), paklava (a pastry), or one of many other Armenian delicacies. Often, too, she would take lap afghans that she had crocheted or large-sized afghans for a couch or a bed to the shut-ins that she visited. Over the years she has crocheted over a thousand beautiful afghans for family members, friends, and others bedridden in hospitals, rest homes, and other facilities, including several hundred baby afghans, some for young mothers with babies in shelters. The list of the recipients of her afghans is long and varied — from college students who received afghans from her in their school colors to The Patriarchate of Jerusalem, His Beatitude Archbishop Torkom Manoogian, when he was the Primate of the Eastern Diocese of the Armenian Church of the United States and Canada. The afghan that she made for him was a large burgundy wool afghan with a gold cross in the center.

The summer that my mother was eighty years old, it was necessary for her to have quint by-pass surgery. During her recovery period at home, after no longer having to be bedridden all day, she began crocheting afghans once again. By Christmas, she had completed six large, very beautiful pastel

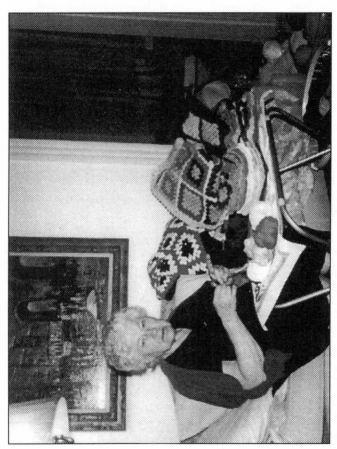

Shnorhig at 80 after her quint by-pass surgery crocheting afghans to sell to make money to send to the orphans in Armenia after the earthquake there.

granny afghans. A group of family members and friends, including the minister of St. James Armenian Apostolic Church in Richmond at the time, Rev. Arsen Barsamian, and his wife were seated around the dining room table marveling at her beautiful work and her remarkable recovery. The conversation turned to the terrible earthquake that had recently occurred in Armenia, as everyone was so grieved over the deaths and destruction there. Mother, particularly, was heartbroken over the situation, saying that she wished that there was some way that she could help the many orphans there, just as she had once been helped so many years before when she too had been an orphan.

Father Barsamian suggested, "Why don't you sell your beautiful afghans and send that money to the Armenian orphans?" His wife agreed, and they insisted on buying two of the afghans that evening as did my brother Richard and his wife Stephanie, who were visiting from New York City; and the last two were bought by Jeanne Saunders, a dear family friend at the table. It was the first time that Mother had ever sold any of her handwork; however, because this was for a worthy cause, she agreed to do so, making $300 for the orphans that evening.

Two local television stations received calls from the minister the next morning, and within days both stations had taped her story and run it on television. The response was incredible, with people calling her from all over the city! In the following months she crocheted and sold so many afghans that she was able to send a check for over $2,000 to Armenia for the orphans of the earthquake by the start of summer.

My mother's Armenian heritage is a very deep part of her, but she is also very proud of being an American citizen. You could say that she thinks of the 4th of July as a second birthday, because that is when she arrived in America and started her new life here. In fact, on the lapels of each of her blazers and coats she always wears one of a beautiful collection of rhinestone American flag pins that my sister assembled for her. It has become a very charming and attractive trademark!

Shmorhig's citizenship picture in November of 1939. She is third from the left.

9

Family Heirlooms and Other Treasures

In a very old and special suitcase at my mother's home are stored family portraits and other treasured photographs. It is a very special suitcase because it is the one that Shnorhig used to bring her few possessions to America. Though somewhat tattered, this faded brown suitcase of a heavy cardboard material is in amazingly good condition for its 73 years. As children we relished pulling this old suitcase out from the back of the closet in my mother's bedroom and pouring over the old photographs within, each with its own wonderful story. Today her grandchildren find these old photographs and their stories just as fascinating as we before them did.

The 1914 photograph of Shnorhig at age 6, a year before the start of the Genocide, with her parents, little sister, and her aunt and uncle.

Though there are many treasured old photographs within, none means as much to any of us as the only photograph that we have of Shnorhig as a child. It was taken in 1914, a year before the Genocide began, when Shnorhig was only six. Her parents, Vartouhi and Hovannes, are in the photograph, as well as her little sister Rosalia. Also in the photograph are Vartouhi's sister Mayrig and her young brother Setrag, who was the student in the seminary in Marash who was burned alive during the Genocide.

The story of how we have possession of this most treasured photograph is a remarkable one. The photograph belonged to Mayrig, a brilliant student who had graduated from the American University in Marash and then had been sent to Germany on a scholarship to get her Masters' degree. Not long in Germany, Mayrig became ill and returned to Marash, as she had contracted cholera, an epidemic having swept through that part of the world. Tragically, she found that she was alone, because all of her family members had either been killed in the Genocide or had left on the Death March. So Mayrig stayed at the Marash orphanage until her death soon afterwards. The matron of the orphanage did something rather amazing; she kept

Mayrig's most treasured possessions: the photograph, a small white purse of Armenian needlelace containing samples of needlelace patterns, and a uniquely beautiful gold ring. It was a 24-carat gold ring made in the shape of delicate butterflies, with an inscription inside of: Love, Vartouhi and Hovannes Keshishian. They had given Mayrig the ring as a graduation gift from college, just prior to having the photograph taken. Ten years later when Shnorhig was sixteen and leaving for America, the matron of the orphanage in Shimlon gave her these special treasures to take with her to America. It was remarkable that in that decade of incalculable destruction that they had been able to keep these very precious keepsakes for her when everything around them was being demolished!

We could spend many hours pouring over other wonderful old photographs that are stored in this special suitcase, but let us go, instead, to the bedroom next to this one where my grandmother's dresser is, because it is full of unique and special heirlooms started by Vartouhi and Shnorhig over seventy years ago when they first came to their new land to begin new lives with little more than memories from the old world.

As we carefully examine the contents of the drawers, we are awestruck at the varied and exquisitely beautiful handwork within. There is the delicate Armenian needlelace, which is now a lost art, made by Vartouhi over the years of her life in America. She was fortunate to have learned to do this rare handwork as a young girl in her orphanage, and over the years of doing this art form in America, she became an expert at creating this delicate lace. Although Shnorhig was not taught any handwork when she was in either orphanage, she did learn to do Armenian needlelace from Vartouhi, but chose another form of needlework to master, becoming an expert at crocheting.

She has spent her life creating a volume of truly magnificent pieces. It began when she first came to America; she used to go to the dime stores and study the pieces pictured in the needlecraft books and then go home and copy them. Basically she taught herself to crochet, picking up a needle and thread and instinctively knowing what to do. She did, however, get some helpful points and patterns from a very sweet lady in Richmond, Hripseme Mardigian. But after copying a number of different designs, she began to create her own, making everything from tablecloths, bedspreads, dresser scarves, placemats, doilies, and coasters, to baby dresses, women's sweaters, and purses. I remember when we were very young children, we had an opportunity to go with my mother to Hyde Park, former President Franklin Delano Roosevelt's home in New York. There my mother particularly liked the bedspread that was in the master bedroom. She studied it carefully for a few moments and then returned home to create that pattern, as well as variations of it in other bedspreads for family members. She was a young woman at the time and felt very proud to have that beautiful crochet pattern from Hyde Park in her own home. There it is, and isn't it beautiful?

But we must not leave this trove of treasures without exploring another drawer of dresser scarves and tablecloths. Made of linen, they have beautiful patterns of pulled threads that are combined with crocheted inserts and trims. Though many of the dresser scarves are very worn from years of wear, they still have as delicate a beauty today as they did many decades ago when Shnorhig was first married and began creating them. Recently I took many of them out of the drawer to admire them and asked Mother to tell me their stories. She told me about each piece, including one piece that was not in the drawer. It was a crocheted piece that she had made when she was in her late 20's for the altar of St. John's Episcopal Church in Richmond, Virginia, where Patrick Henry had made his famous speech of "Give me liberty, or give me death" just prior to the start of the Revolutionary War. Our family attended that beautiful, old historic church at the time that she had crocheted the altar piece, my brother Marshall being one of the altar boys. At the end of our exploration of those beautiful pieces, my mother said to me with so much contentment in her voice: "God loves me so much. He gave me the ability to crochet. It has been such a wonderful activity for me to have all of my life. I am so lucky to have had this gift."

Her deep appreciation of this gift has always been shown in her generous sharing of her work with others. A good example of this occurred when my mother was in her fifties and she read in the newspaper that the Needlework Guild of America would be meeting in a church nearby for the Richmond community. The goal was to bring needlework to the gathering, and at Thanksgiving it would be included with food and new clothing for the needy. She took two pieces of her work to the meeting and has continued contributing to those who are in need. In fact, when she was 85, she was the Chairlady for the Needlework Guild of America for St. Mark's Episcopal Church's Women's Group, and they assembled hundreds of pieces of new clothing and needlework for needy people in the Richmond, Virginia, area. Now she is continuing this work by crocheting as many lap afghans as she can, calling them knee warmers, for those in the community who are housebound.

Reluctantly we leave these precious family heirlooms and make our way down the winding staircase to the entryway downstairs, and our eyes fall on what I consider a truly special treasure. It is one of a pair of exquisite old rocking chairs that are 66 years old. The other chair has found its place in a small room between the living room and the dining room, called, appropriately, "the little room." They became part of our family when my brother Yervant was a year old and my mother was expecting my sister. Given to my parents by Dan and Santookht Akullian when they visited my parents from Albany, New York, they felt that my mother and father needed the rocking chairs, with two small children and another on the way. How right they were! We have loved them and used them extensively over the years, so many children, grandchildren, and great-grandchildren being rocked to sleep in one or the other of the chairs.

Delicately carved of walnut that has achieved a gentle patina over the years, these beautiful old rockers are large, but graceful in style. They went through an extraordinary transformation about twenty years ago when they were renovated because of my mother's new-found talent of needlepoint. For many years she had admired needlepoint, but had considered it too expensive a hobby for her to have. As she was approaching her 70th birthday, however, she decided that she must explore this beautiful art form further, so she went to the needlecraft store that was nearby and took a few lessons in needlepoint. In no time she had mastered the art and has now done close to one hundred pieces in the last twenty years. Two of her earliest pieces were the seats of the two upholstered rocking chairs. The seat of one is a light grey background with pastel flowers, and the back of the rocker is grey velvet. The needlepoint of the other rocker is a rich copper-colored background with delicate flowers, and the back of that rocker is a copper velvet. On the back of each rocker is a small crocheted piece made by Shnorhig. These two old rocking chairs are truly exquisite pieces that each of us in the family

Shnorhig doing the needlepoint for her rocking chairs.

treasures so very much. But we must now continue our journey through my mother's home because there is so much more to discover.

As we walk into the living room, we quickly notice a crocheted piece in a frame on the wall. It was made by Shnorhig almost forty years ago for a very dear friend of hers, Zarouhi Deloian, as a wedding gift. A few years ago she generously returned it, saying that it should remain in our family for the children and grandchildren to enjoy, just as she had for so many years. Looking at the opposite wall, we notice a pale blue piece of Armenian needlelace, also in a frame. It was done by my grandmother when she was 79 years old. A few months before her death, she had almost completed it when she said to her daughter, "Shnorhig, I can't do this anymore. Wait until I am gone, and then you finish it." After her death Shnorhig completed the piece for her. It has become a very special treasure in our family.

The walls of my mother's living room hold many treasures that are originals. In fact, there is yet another unique one: the Armenian alphabet in counted cross-stitch. The story of its origin is truly a remarkable one. It came about because of a misfortune that my mother had when visiting my brother Richard in upstate New York almost 16 years ago. There was a robbery in his home and her four rings were taken. She was heartbroken, most of all because her engagement ring and wedding band were among the rings lost. She had been widowed for fifteen years and felt that those two rings were among her most valued possessions. Another ring that had been taken that meant so much to her was an exquisite gold ring with a very large, beautiful opal stone. This ring meant a great deal to her because the stone had been cut by her only surviving brother Avedis.

Shnorhig returned home to Virginia very sad about the loss of her rings. At the time she had only four grandchildren, and she had always had it in her mind to leave each of them one of her rings, as she had no heirlooms from the old country to leave them.

A few days after her return, a very close family friend, Frances Sullivan, came to visit her, and they talked of the loss of the rings and her deep disappointment. As they sat in the living room, Frances asked her what she could do to help her. Mother answered, "Thank you, Frances, but there's nothing anyone can do. When I feel a little better, I'm going to the needlecraft store on Cary Street and ask if they know of a college student in art who might be able to make a pattern of the Armenian alphabet for me so that I can make it in needlework for my grandchildren." Frances then asked if she had a picture of the Armenian alphabet that she might see. Mother showed her a paper placemat showing the alphabet. Her dear friend asked to borrow it for a few days and then left. The next day she stopped by with a draft, which was a perfect replica of the alphabet! My mother and sister were amazed. A few days later she returned with the alphabet completed in counted cross-stitch and beautifully framed and gave it to my mother, who was overwhelmed with this priceless gift! The draft was then sent to the Diocese of the Armenian Church in New York City, and from there the first one thousand copies were made to be available to Armenians all over the United States and Canada to purchase and complete for their own homes. Frances very generously prepared framed replicas of the Armenian alphabet for all five of Mother's children, but the original is proudly hanging in Shnorhig's living room. In fact, throughout my mother's home are beautiful pieces of Frances Sullivan's unique handwork that each of us in the family enjoys and values so much.

It is time now to make our way into the dining room because the wonderful aroma from the kitchen is beckoning us to the long table already covered with numerous Armenian delicacies. Is that freshly baked Armenian pita bread, a favorite of all of her grandchildren, or is it cheoregs, an Armenian biscuit often shaped as braids? We are lucky to have both of them, as Shnorhig is an expert baker who indulges us frequently with her baking. There are black olives and tourshoo (Armenian pickles); <u>everyone</u> agrees that my mother is the best in the making of tourshoo! Feta cheese and Armenian string cheese are part of the spread too, of course, and aren't we lucky because there is lahmejoun (Armenian meat pizza) and beoreg (Armenian turnovers made of a mixture of either cheese, ground lamb or beef).

Though today's feast is strictly Armenian food, we grew up eating a very varied cuisine — everything from Waldolf salad, chili, and lasagna, to apple pie and those very special fruitcakes at Christmas. But let us enjoy our spread of superb Armenian food today. And as we do, I must tell you the most extraordinary story of all. It concerns that large bowl of madzoon, because it is my family's most unique treasure. It is one of my grandmother's greatest legacies to our family. It began when she came to America in 1921 from Cyprus. On that journey she brought with her some magart (the starter to make madzoon). Upon her arrival in America, she made madzoon from that magart, and it has remained in our family for over 75 years! Every week my grandmother made madzoon from the previous week's magart. After my mother was married, she got magart from her mother, and she has never let the process stop, making madzoon each week — to the present time! Those two ladies have given hundreds of people magart in the past 75 years from that starter brought by Vartouhi from Cyprus to America. The common practice, for many people, has been to make madzoon for a period of time, finish it, and then in a few years to get magart from someone and start the process again. But these two ladies have kept part of the Old World alive by never letting that original magart end, making, what I believe, is a truly extraordinary experience when one eats madzoon at my mother's home!

It is about time that we complete our Armenian "snack" with some Armenian coffee and paklava, a world-famous dessert. There are an assortment of beautiful demitasse cups from which we can select, each with its own special story, some going back to my grandmother's early days of marriage in America. The gold set with flowers in jewel tones is truly magnificent, a gift from a young Armenian couple that my parents helped when they were first married. The beautiful old china closet that houses the demitasse cups has a story of its own to tell. It was a wedding gift to my father and mother over seventy years ago. This came about because three Armenian men were in a dispute over an apartment building that they had bought together. My father found them an attorney and functioned as their interpreter in court. The problem of the apartment building was resolved to their satisfaction, and to show their appreciation to my father for his help in putting this unpleasant matter behind them, they sent this beautiful china closet and an icebox to my father and mother as a wedding gift. All of their grandchildren would love to have this wonderful old china closet someday, but it will not be soon, because its delicate doors are opened frequently as demitasse cups are brought out for Shnorhig to have Armenian coffee with her friends, Zarouhi Deloian and Marian Minasian, and her daughter Rose, (and this daughter Flo as well when I am visiting!). For many years, Shnorhig had weekly visits and lunches with Zarouhi and Marian's mother, Anna DerKrikorian, enjoying her close friendship with her dear friend until her death.

While walking through my mother's home, perhaps you saw the small, porcelain praying hands night light in her bedroom or the beautiful plate of that theme in the entry hall or the cross-stitch of praying hands done by her granddaughter Donna in the little room next to the living room. It is because the theme of praying hands flows gently throughout her home, one of her many ways of expressing her deep faith in God. I remember recently when her two young grandsons, Damien and Adrian, noticed images of praying hands in her home and then went through the house to discover each one, just as their two older sisters, Sari and Marisa, had done many years before.

The beautiful gold butterfly ring is gone too, lost somewhere in the house many years ago when my brothers and sister were small. Though that very special ring from the Old World is gone, the wonderful madzoon remains. And all of the remarkable heirlooms created over the years by two remarkable women remain as well.

Photographs of Shnorhig and Zadoor taken in 1935 to be used as passport pictures for a trip to France in order to see Zadoor's youngest brother who was a student there. The trip was never taken because his brother died of tuberculosis that year, having been in very poor health from his experiences during the Genocide.

10

The Strength to Survive

What was it about Shnorhig, her mother Vartouhi, and her grandfather that made them survivors? Why didn't they give up in the face of all of the horror of the Genocide? How is it that they did not become bitter?

If you ask Shnorhig those questions today, her answers come from her deep and enduring religious faith. As the primary source of her answers, she cites Romans 8:28: "All things work for the good for those that love the Lord." In her own words, paraphrased as: "Even when bad things happen to you, if you hold on to your faith in God, your belief in Him, and your love for Him, ultimately things will work out for your good. You must have patience and believe in Him." She feels that, as in the Book of Job, she cannot question God as to why they had to go through the Genocide, saying: "God had a purpose. I trust Him. We may never know why we were chosen for that ordeal. Yet something good came out of my being an orphan, as I got an excellent education in the Armenian language as well as my religious convictions that I would not have had otherwise. As Paul said, 'In every suffering, there is a reward.' "

Shnorhig believes with all of her being that it was God who saved her and her mother. She describes many incidents to support her belief, one concerning a time during the Genocide when she might have drowned, but didn't. It was during the period when she was struggling to survive alone on the streets. She was very thirsty and finally found a water wheel. As she lay down drinking the water, Turkish men came up from behind, picked her up, and cursing at her threw the terrified little girl into the canal. Not knowing how to swim, she screamed and struggled in the water, somehow miraculously getting herself to the water wheel. She held on to it for a long time until finally a sympathetic person walking by saw her and pulled her out of the canal, saving her life.

Another incident she cites was during the journey of the orphans from the orphanage in Marash to the orphanage in Shimlon, just outside of Beirut. It was during the first part of the journey when the orphans were travelling by foot that something terrifying happened to her. Shnorhig with two other little orphans briefly left the group to relieve themselves, as was the practice to do. On their way back to join the group, they were discovered by several Turkish men with donkeys carrying loads of wood. They cursed at the girls, beat them brutally, and finally kicked them off the side of the mountainous road, the children falling about 50 feet down the mountain. Screaming, crying, and terrified, they began to try to climb back up the mountain. Fortunately, the "Father" of the orphanage noticed that several of the little girls were missing from the group. He and some of the older girls went back to search, heard their screams, and helped them back up the mountain. All three of the children were badly hurt from the beating and fall but had to continue on the long journey. By the time that they had walked to Halab, gotten on an open train to Beirut, and then been taken by trucks to Shimlon, Shnorhig was in great pain and very ill. She had an extremely high fever, and her tongue was badly swollen. An

Armenian matron at the orphanage, Hyganoush Bagi, who knew Vartouhi, comforted Shnorhig, telling her not to be afraid, that she would care for her as her own mother would. She instructed her to eat a certain kind of grass that would hurt her very much and cause her tongue to bleed, telling her that she must do this for as many weeks as necessary to clear up the infection. She stayed on this agonizing treatment until she was completely healed.

The strength of her grandfather's and mother's deep religious convictions enabled them to endure unendurable atrocities and to continue to live with courage and unwavering faith in God and in life. They are the positive role models that Shnorhig remembers as vividly as the pain of the horrific sights and traumas that she witnessed and survived. This was the legacy that they gave this small child, enabling her to live through those horrible years and in the process evolve into the strong, spiritual individual that she became — a survivor.

Their deep religious faith and the wisdom of the Bible gave them the understanding needed to live life in a positive way. Vartouhi and Shnorhig — two ordinary women leading extraordinary lives — turned their horrendous decade of pain into a lifetime of helping fellow human beings to live better

Shnorhig today.

Olan Mills Photography

lives, because they had the courage to turn tragedy into triumph.

Vartouhi, my grandmother, is no longer with us, as she passed away 26 years ago, when she was near 80. She had been failing for weeks after years of being ill. My mother and sister were at her bedside, and she said quietly to them, "Don't be afraid

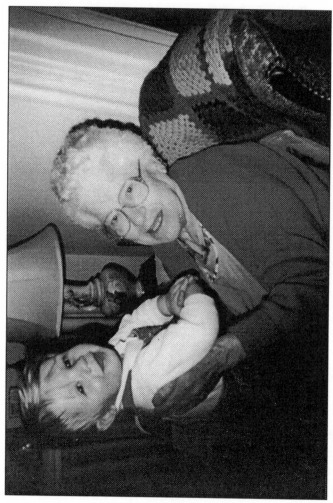

Shmorhig and her youngest great-grandchild Jacob in one of their daily happy "visits" together.

or call the doctor. It is time for me to go. The angels are here singing to take me with them." She then began to sing a religious song very softly and within moments, as my sister held her, she died peacefully with a beautiful smile on her face.

My mother Shnorhig, at 89, continues to reach out to others less fortunate than she. Each morning she begins the day by reading the Bible and other Christian works. Then she has the immense pleasure of the company of her youngest great-grandchild, her precious little Jacob, who is her granddaughter Donna's baby son. This is possible because my sister Rose is his nanny! The two have wonderful little "visits" together, each delighting the other, as Shnorhig is busy much of the day crocheting afghans for those who are ill or elderly shut-ins at home, in hospitals, or other facilities. She gives at least two afghans a month (sometimes four!) to her ladies' group at St. Mark's Episcopal Church in Richmond, Virginia, to give to elderly shut-ins in the area. The ladies in her group proudly and lovingly call her "Amazing Grace."

How wise of them. "Amazing Grace" indeed. A name that well describes this remarkable woman who has spent her entire life trying to comfort those in pain.

11

Living One's Faith

During and after the Genocide, Vartouhi and Shnorhig's faith in God was intensified, and the gift of wisdom came from their experiences. We, the beneficiaries of their wisdom, are forever grateful, because through their actions and their words, those of us who have known them have learned many valuable lessons about life.

First and foremost, their faith in a higher power — their enduring faith in God — made it possible for them to survive the unspeakable ordeals that they had to confront in their lives — without ever giving up. Vartouhi lost her first husband in the Genocide and her two youngest children starved to death. For a few years she lived in the painful state of not knowing if her only other child was still alive. She lost her second husband at age 54; then at age 70 she was devastated when Vartan, the older of her two sons born in America from her second marriage, died a painful and agonizing death of lung cancer, at age 39 and the time when his only child, Talitha Victoria, was about to be born. Vartouhi was almost 80 when she died, living nine more years after that horrible tragedy. She was able to endure the tragedies of her life because she never lost her faith in God. That faith is where Vartouhi and Shnorhig got their enormous strength, that made them wonderful role models for so many fortunate people.

Once when talking together about the pains and struggles of life, Vartouhi had told Shnorhig that each day one must pray to God for help and guidance, not expecting that the specific problem of the moment will immediately be resolved. She had said: "It is a mistake to think that God has not heard our prayers when the problem has not gone away, because God works in his own time and in his own way. We must not question his wisdom. Look at us. We suffered terribly and lost everything, just as Job suffered and lost everything. But we have so much now. I have you and two sons and five grandchildren. God did not forsake us, nor did he forsake Job. He gave him more than he had had before. That's why we must pray each day, no matter what is happening in our lives and keep our faith in God and his infinite wisdom."

Shnorhig was asked at age 85 to give a talk about the Genocide to the senior citizens' group at St. Mark's Episcopal Church in Richmond, Virginia. After her talk, there was a question and answer period where she was asked the question: "After all of the horror of the Genocide, how have you been able to become such a normal, well-adjusted and happy, productive person?" In her answer she first told the story of a young American soldier who, after serving in the Philippines, had returned home and met a girl he fell in love with and wanted to marry. Before they could marry and fulfill their dreams of building a house by the river, the young man noticed on his arms and shoulders some strange spots. The doctor that he saw had also been in the Philippines and knew immediately that it was leprosy — shocking the young couple and shattering their dreams and plans. The doctor told him that he could give up and die or fight it and go on.

The young man went away for treatment, learning that he must live in isolation, avoiding

Shnorhig at 85 with her daughter Rose with whom she lives.

contact with everyone. Despair enveloped him again. But this time it was short-lived: he decided to return to the Philippines to a leper colony. There he took a new course in life. He not only gave the other lepers hope and courage, but he spent the next 25 years of his life making the once-dreary place into a productive, healthy environment. Fisheries were established, a power station built, and abundant gardens for healthy eating were created. Some of the lepers even recovered and went home! Though the man in question did not, he died peacefully, knowing that his life had not been in vain, for he had created a new dream and fulfilled it by making life better and more meaningful for many others. The story, told by Rev. Harry M. Missirlian in *Treasures in Earthen Vessels*, is one of many inspirational essays that my mother reads each day, this book being her favorite of its kind. In the essay in question, Rev. Missirlian had briefly paraphrased the story that is told in Perry Burgess's book, *Who Walk Alone*, in order to make a powerful spiritual point.

Then Shnorhig went to the Bible, speaking of Paul's asking God for his help, his answer being: "My grace is enough for you." Moses was told the same, showing how merciful God is, that he does not give you a problem too big to handle. She ended her answer by reading the eloquent "A Christmas Prayer", penned anonymously by a confederate soldier over a century ago. He wrote:

I asked God for strength, that I might achieve,
I was made weak, that I might learn humbly to obey.
I asked for health, that I might do greater things,
I was given infirmity, that I might do better things.
I asked for riches, that I might be happy,
I was given poverty that I might be wise.
I asked for power that I might have the praise of men,
I was given weakness, that I might feel the need of God.
I asked for all things, that I might enjoy life,
I was given life, that I might enjoy all things.
I got nothing that I asked for — but everything I had hoped for,
Almost despite myself, my unspoken prayers were answered.
I am among all men, most richly blessed.

Shnorhig ended her reading of this prayer by saying that when we truly understand the meaning of receiving, then we are released to become true givers. Her talk, which was to be a half-hour, had become an hour and fifteen minutes.

Throughout their lives, both Vartouhi and Shnorhig tried to remain calm and hopeful, no matter what was happening to them. During the Genocide, they searched for food, tried to stay alive, attempting to help those around them in any way that they could. They were physically tortured and hurt, but nothing could dim the spirit within. Examining the lives of both women during and after the Genocide, we see their refusal to give up — always having hope, no matter what horror they might be facing. Those around them have been strengthened and inspired to do the same. One never truly gets over traumas of the magnitude of the Genocide; it always remains within the psyche of the person. But both women were better able to live with those horrible memories by coming out of themselves through the helping of others.

As far back as I can remember, both my mother and my grandmother used verses from the Bible and other inspirational readings to help others, as well as themselves, cope with the difficulties and hurts of life. Rev. Missirlian's wonderful book, *Treasures In Earthen Vessels*, is one that she reads each day because of its format of using stories about different kinds of people contronting problems in various life situations that always teach us lessons and values. I remember her helping my brother Richard handle his disappointment of not getting a fellowship to the University of London and at the same time giving him hope for something better for him in the future. Within a few months, "something better" came to him in the form of a fellowship to study at the University of Edinburgh, followed by a year at the Sorbonne. "When one door closes, God will make sure that another opens" she had wisely told him.

Another situation illustrating Shnorhig's ability to find answers in the Bible for dealing with life's disappointments was the matter of the loss of her rings by theft. Though she was hurt and troubled by the loss, she attempted in a calm way to make things better, the result being that her idea of the Armenian alphabet being created in cross-stitch became a reality through the talent and generosity of her compassionate friend, Frances Sullivan. Truly not only a greater gift and legacy to leave her grandchildren and great-grandchildren than her rings would have been, but also a treasured gift for Armenians throughout the United States and the world, to be valued and appreciated and handed down to their grandchildren and great-grandchildren also. As she explains, "All things work for the good for them that love the Lord."

I remember as a child overhearing the remnants of a conversation that my grandmother had had with someone about a package that she was sending to her relatives in South America. It was a very expensive Bible, and the person had warned her that she was taking a risk — that the Bible might never reach its destination, as there was the chance that it could be stolen or lost. My grandmother had smiled gently, saying that that would not be a problem, for it would mean that the person who had gotten the Bible needed it far more than the relatives to whom she was sending it. "God works in mysterious ways," she had said.

Sometimes Shnorhig uses humor to impart wisdom, because my father to whom she was married for almost forty years until his death was a master at doing that. The wisdom that Zadoor imparted to his children and others was philosophical but almost always in a comic venue. He was a masterful storyteller, knowing dozens and dozens of wonderful stories about a comic Armenian character named Hogah, a country bumpkin with a wife and a tremendous talent for getting into a hilarious jam, yet a predicament that always taught a lesson about life. On occasion Shnorhig will attempt to tell a Hogah story, if she can control her laughter enough to complete it!

My mother is so thankful for her blessings. I have heard her say so many times: "God loves me so much. He's given me so much in my life. I'm the luckiest person in the whole world." Recently in her doctor's office she exclaimed to him, "I have the five most wonderful children any mother could ever have." She adores her grandchildren as much as her children, encouraging all of them, as she did with her own children, to discover and develop their talents. For example, she was the person who guided her oldest grandchild Larry into the Junior Curator Program at the Virginia Museum of Fine Arts in Richmond, as well as involvement with the Math and Science Center in the area. Her two oldest grandchildren, Larry and Donna, are successful, productive adults because of her daily guidance and influence in their upbringing. And just last week she said to my sister, "I feel so blessed that God has given me great-grandchildren. I could never have believed that I could have lived so long and been blessed in this way."

Recently I made a new discovery about my gentle mother that truly touched me. As I was watching her busy in her daily activity of crocheting afghans for shut-ins, most of them people that she will never meet, I admired the one that she was working on as well as several others that she had recently completed, specifically commenting on the vivid colors and beautiful and unusual color combinations that she always creates. She looked up from her work and said something so moving that I know that it will always be with me. She told me of the tremendous joy that she feels as she is making the bright-colored afghans for shut-ins because, in her words: "Not only will it give them warmth, but it will cheer them too, just as the brightly-colored ribbons for our hair cheered me and all of the other girls in the orphanage many, many years ago and made us feel so pretty and special. It made us feel that someone cared. It brightened our lives; it made us feel that we mattered."

My mother knows the secret of the joy of life. It thrills her to see the first rose that blooms in her garden. Sitting on her sunporch crocheting in the early morning and feeling the first rays of the sun peeping through the partially-drawn blinds and hearing the birds chirping in her garden gives her great contentment. A baby's smile and cooing gives her the greatest of delights. Enjoying a wonderful meal with loved ones, seeing the varied beauties of nature on a drive, her daily reading of the Bible and other inspirational readings fill her heart with joy. She is indeed blessed. "And we know that all things work together for good to them that love God, to them who are the called according to his purpose." Romans: 8:28.

Epilogue

Very few people from Zeitoun survived the Armenian Genocide of 1915, because the Turks burned their land after killing almost everyone there. The people of Zeytoon fought very hard and are revered by Armenians all over the world for their courage and spirit.

On the other side of the world from Zeitoun, in my patio in Pacifica, California, there is a small olive tree. While it has a fragile look, I know that it is strong and hearty. Over the years it has survived many heavy rains and hurricane-like winds but has continued to stand strong in its delicate beauty.

Each time I gaze at my olive tree, I am reminded of my mother and my grandmother, both small and delicate in stature, yet possessing a faith at once miraculous and invincible. A deep love and admiration fills my heart.

I look at my olive tree, and I know that my family members 80 years ago did not suffer and die in vain. They live on. In that olive tree. In my heart and soul. And in the hearts and souls of all people everywhere who believe in the dignity of all human beings.

Bibliography

Douglas, John M. *The Armenians*. New York: J. J. Winthrop Corp., 1992.

Missirlian, Harry M. *Treasures in Earthen Vessels*. California: The Armenian Evangelical Union of North America, 1988.

Morgenthau, Henry. *Ambassador Morganthau's Story*. 1918. Reprint, New York: New Age Publishers, 1975.

Soghoian, Grace. Personal interview as distilled over a lifetime of conversations. Richmond, Virginia.

Toynbee, Arnold Joseph, 1989-1975. *Armenian Atrocities: The Murder of a Nation* by Arnold Toynbee. With a speech delivered by Lord Bryce in the House of Lords. New York: Tankian Publishing Co., 1975.

.